The BOOK of HEIRLOOMS

The BOOK of HEIRLOOMS

Needlework treasures and how to create them

Julia Jones

PREMIER EDITIONS

To Ken Ames for his unfailing good advice and unceasing encouragement

Published in 1996 by Premier Editions
An Imprint of Merehurst Limited
Ferry House, 51-57 Lacy Road, Putney, London SW15 1PR

ISBN 1-897730-14-4

A catalogue record of this book is available from the British Library.

Edited by **Vivienne Wells**

Designed by **Sara Kidd**

Photography by **Anna Hodgson**

Styling by **Clare Louise Hunt**

Illustrations by **Alex Harwood and Brihton Illustration**

Colour separation by P&W Graphics Pte Ltd, Singapore

Printed by Tien Wah Press (Pte) Ltd, Singapore

Contents

INTRODUCTION

From time to time, each of us will celebrate an occasion which is unique and very personal. It would seem appropriate, therefore, to mark such special events by the making of a gift or gifts, endowed with a little of our own spirit - gifts that will carry the hopes and good wishes of the giver and will reinforce the precious bond of love. The projects in this book have been designed to do just that, marking all the milestones of a full and happy life.

Each chapter includes two or three projects, all graded by a system of symbols into three categories: simple, intermediate or more complex. The projects become progressively more time consuming and so an approximate guide to the length of time required for each one is also given, as shown opposite. This will, of course, merely provide a rough guideline. Do not be concerned if you find that you take more or less time.

Beginner's projects should take a maximum of 10 hours to complete, putting them in range of even the busiest craftsperson. Some readers will, on the other hand, be prepared to spend many weeks producing a special gift which could truly be described as an 'heirloom'. Whatever your skill level, all the projects featured in this book have been carefully thought out and chosen to offer items which will be admired and treasured for generations. I hope that you will enjoy making and giving these gifts as much as I have enjoyed creating them for you.

Julia Jones, 1996

The tradition of giving handmade gifts can be traced back for centuries, through every civilization and class structure. As a girl, Queen Elizabeth I of England took up her needle to produce individual and expressive gifts for her family and friends. In 1544, the young Princess is said to have made an embroidered book cover as a New Year's gift for her step-mother, Katharine Parr. The making of personal gifts has never been purely the domain of the rich. From the needlepoint slippers and hand-whittled lace bobbins of the 18th and 19th century, to today's cross-stitch greetings cards, the pleasure derived by both the giver and recipient surely makes the time and effort involved well worth while.

Guide to project symbols

❦ beginner's project, which can be tackled with confidence by those new to the craft

❦❦ project for those with a working knowledge of the craft

❦❦❦ project suitable only for those with a good knowledge of the skills required, or for those with access to help and advice

❧ project should take no more than 10 hours to complete

❧❧ project should take between 25 and 40 hours to complete

❧❧❧ project may take in excess of 40 hours to complete

THE BIRTH OF A CHILD

The birth of a child is an important occasion for any family, and is often marked by the making of traditional items of clothing for a christening or other religious celebration. Mothers, grandmothers, aunts and godmothers will all be keen to provide something for a special baby.

CROCHETED LACE SUMMER BONNET IN FINE COTTON

The two exquisite bonnets featured here will prove a delightful addition to baby's outfit, whatever the occasion. White cotton thread has been used to produce a fresh and dainty lace bonnet (the lower one in the photograph), ideal for keeping baby's head cool on balmy summer days. Easy to launder, enabling it to be worn again and again, it will surely be treasured for generations to come. *The fine silk bonnet in ivory is described on page 14.*

MATERIALS

one 50g ball (1¾oz) Coats Opera cotton no. 5 in white
1.5mm (UK size 2½/US size 6) steel crochet hook
1m (1yd) double-faced 12 mm (½in)-wide satin ribbon in white

TENSION
6 pattern rows to 5cm/1in

ABBREVIATIONS
For complete list of abbreviations and US conversions, see page 122

Make a chain of 162 sts.

Row 1: 1 dc [sc] into 2nd ch from hook ⋆1 ch, miss 3 ch, 5 tr [dc] into next ch, 1 ch, miss 3 ch, 1 dc [sc] into next ch; rep from ⋆ ending with 4 ch, turn; (number of shells - 20);

Row 2: (this will be the right side of the work) ⋆1 tr [dc] into each of the next 2 tr [dc], into the next tr [dc] work 1 tr [dc] 2ch 1 tr [dc], 1 tr [dc] into each of next 2 tr [dc]; rep from ⋆ ending with 1 dbl tr [tr] into next dc [sc], 1 ch, turn;

Row 3: 1 dc [sc] into the first dbl tr [tr], 3 ch, ⋆1 dc [sc] into next 2 ch lp, 7 ch; rep from ⋆ ending with 1 dc [sc] into last 2 ch lp, 3 ch, 1 dc [sc] into 4th of 4 ch, 1 ch, turn;
Row 4: 1 dc [sc] into first dc [sc] into next 3 ch lp, ⋆1 dc [sc] into next dc [sc], 7 dc [sc] into next 7 ch lp; rep from ⋆ ending with 1 dc [sc] into next dc [sc], 3 dc [sc] into next 3 ch lp, 1 dc [sc] into next dc [sc], 3 ch, turn;

Row 5: Miss first.dc [sc], 1 tr [dc] into each dc [sc], 1 ch, turn;

Row 6: 1 dc [sc] into each tr [dc], 1 dc [sc] into 3rd of 3 ch, 1 ch, turn;

Row 7: 1 dc [sc] into first dc [sc], ⋆1 ch, miss 3 dc [sc], 5 tr [dc] into next dc [sc], 1 ch, miss 3 dc [sc], 1 dc [sc] into next dc [sc]; rep from ⋆ ending with 4 ch, turn.

Rep rows 2-7 twice more, then

Chain stitch (a)

Chain stitch (b)

rows 2-6 once again, but omit turning ch at end of final row. Fasten off.

Crown panel

Row 1: With wrong side of work facing, miss first 56 dc [sc] (7 shells) and attach thread to next dc [sc], 1 dc [sc] into same place as before, *1 ch, miss 3 dc [sc], 5 tr [dc] into next dc [sc], 1 ch, miss 3 dc [sc], 1 dc [sc] into next dc [sc]; rep from * 5 times more (6 shells), 4 ch, turn;

Rep rows 2-7 of main section 3 times more, then rows 2-6 again, omitting turning ch at end of last row. Fasten off. Slipstitch seams together.

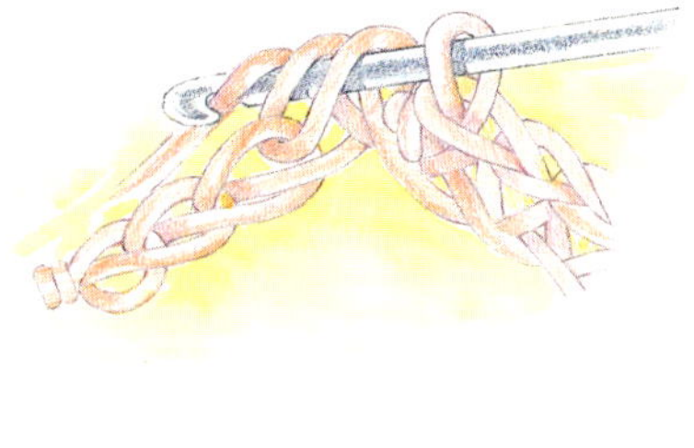

Double crochet (single crochet) (a)

Double crochet (single crochet) (b)

Double crochet (single crochet) (c)

Front edging

Row 1: With wrong side of work facing, attach thread to the base of the last dc [sc] made on row 1, 1 dc [sc] into same place as before, 2 ch, 3 tr [dc] into next sp, *into next sp work 1 dc [sc] 2 ch and 3 tr [dc]; rep from * along front edge ending with 1 dc [sc] into base of last dc [sc], do not fasten off.

Crochet has been popular for baby garments since the 19th century. In Victorian England, crochet lace was particularly fashionable; being relatively quick and easy to work, it proved an ideal alternative to the more labour-intensive bobbin and needlelaces of the 17th and 18th centuries. The art of crochet developed in the convents and manor houses of Europe and, along with several other forms of handicrafts, was known as 'nun's work' or white work. Early forms of fine crochet took their inspiration from the designs of 17th century Venetian needlepoint and English Honiton bobbin lace. By 1850 this new crochet was widely exhibited in the fashion capitals of the world, eagerly sought by the rich and famous as the most chic of adornments. To store the completed bonnets wrap them in acid-free tissue paper. Wash the bonnets carefully by hand in a weak solution of mild soapflakes dissolved in tepid water. If in any doubt about washing your own choice of yarn, however, seek the advice of your stockist or a reputable dry cleaner.

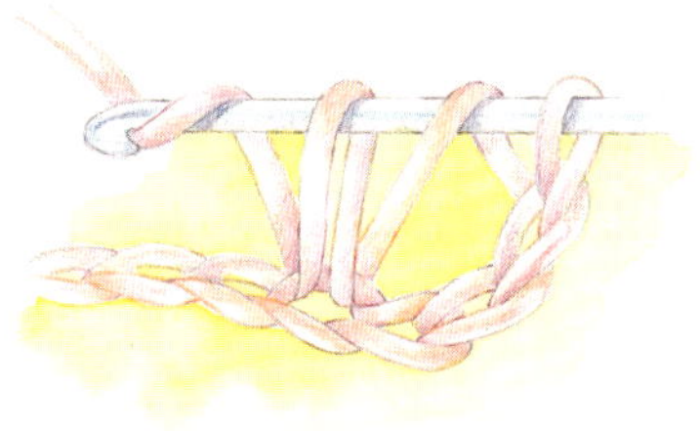

Treble crochet (double crochet) (a)

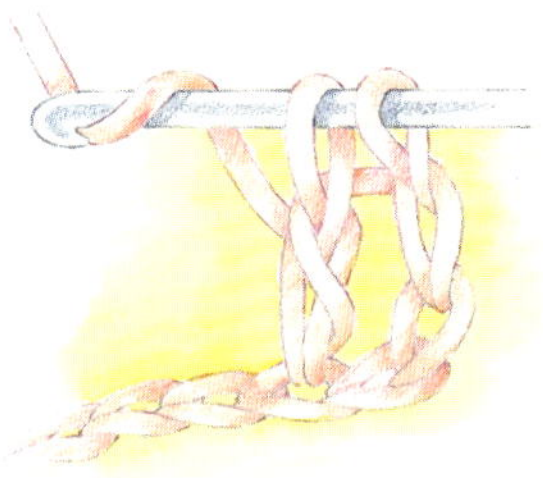

Treble crochet (double crochet) (b)

Treble crochet (double crochet) (c)

Lower edging (continuing with working thread)

Row 1: Work 25 dc [sc] evenly along row-ends of main section to seam, 1 dc [sc] into seam, 22 dc [sc] along back panel to next seam, 1 dc [sc] into seam, 25 dc [sc] along row ends of main section working last dc [sc] into same place as first st on front edging, 3 ch, turn;

Row 2: Miss 1st dc [sc], 1 tr [dc] into next dc [sc], *3ch, miss 2 dc [sc], 1 tr [dc] into each of next 2 dc [sc]; rep from * ending with 1 ch, turn;

Row 3: 1 dc [sc] into 1st tr [dc], 1 dc [sc] between last and next tr [dc], * 3 dc [sc] into next lp, 1 dc [sc] between next 2 sts; rep from * ending with 1 dc [sc] into 3rd of 3 ch, 1 ch, turn;

Row 4: 1 dc [sc] into each dc [sc]. Fasten off.

Finishing: Using a damp cloth and hot iron, gently press bonnet into shape. Press ribbon and thread through the holes of lower edging.

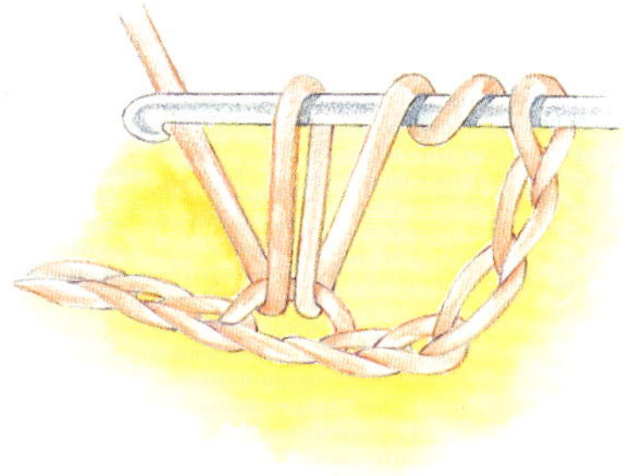

Double treble crochet (treble) (a)

Double treble crochet (treble) (b)

CROCHETED BONNET IN FINE SILK

The silk thread used to make this very special christening bonnet is soft and delicate. It will tone beautifully with the natural shades of pure wool and linen often used for shawls and christening robes, giving a truly traditional appeal to the occasion. Silk thread is slightly more difficult to work than its cotton equivalent. It is very soft and needs to be kept at an even tension, and it also has a tendency to split whilst being worked, but these are minor difficulties which, with careful working, can easily be overcome. Silk is, of course, more expensive than mass-produced cotton threads, but for a special baby the extra outlay is surely more than justified. You are, after all, making a family heirloom, to be cherished through future generations.

MATERIALS

6 spools of medium-weight silk thread (XM 20/3) in ivory (see supplier list on page 125 or 50g (1¾ oz) thread of your choice)
1.5mm (UK size 2½/US size 6) steel crochet hook
1m (1yd) double-faced 12mm(½in)-wide satin ribbon in ivory

TENSION
4 pattern rows to 5cm/1in

ABBREVIATIONS
See page 122.

Make a chain of 162 sts.

Row 1: (right side) 1 dc [sc] into 2nd ch from hook *, miss 4 ch, leaving last lp of each on hook, work 2 trip tr [dble tr] into next ch, thread over and draw through all lps on hook (a 2 trip tr cl [2 dble tr cl] made), 3 ch, into same ch work a 2 trip tr cl [2 dble tr cl] 3 ch and a 2 trip tr cl [2 dble tr cl] miss 4 ch, 1 dc [sc] into next ch; rep from * to end, 5 ch, turn (18 shells);

Row 2: 1 trip tr [dble tr] into first dc [sc], *3 ch, 1 dc [sc] into next lp, 2ch, 1 dc [sc] into next lp, 3 ch, a 2 trip tr cl [2 dble tr cl] into next dc [sc]; rep from * to end, 1 ch, turn;

Row 3: 1 dc [sc] into first cl, *1 dc [sc] into next lp, into next 2 ch lp work (a 2 trip tr cl [2 dble tr cl], 3 ch) twice and a 2 trip tr cl [2 dble tr cl], 1 dc [sc] into next lp, 2 ch; rep from * omitting 2 ch at end of last rep, 1 dc [sc] into 4th of 5 ch, 5 ch, turn;

Row 4: 1 trip tr [dble tr] into first dc [sc], *3 ch, 1 dc [sc] into next lp, 2 ch, 1 dc [sc] into next lp, 3 ch, a 2 trip trl cl [2 dble tr cl] into next 2 ch lp; rep from * working last cl into last dc, 1 ch, turn.

Rep rows 3 and 4 a further 8 times (10 completed shells in all), ending with row 4. Fasten off and cut yarn.

Crown panel

Row 1: With right side of work facing, miss first 60 dc [sc] (6 shells) and attach thread to next dc [sc], 1 dc [sc] into same place as before, ⋆1 dc [sc] into next lp, into next 2 ch lp work (a 2 trip tr cl [2 dble tr cl], 3 ch) twice and a 2 trip tr cl [2 dble tr cl], 1 dc [sc] into next lp, 2 ch; rep from ⋆, omitting 2 ch at end of last rep, 1 dc [sc] into 5th of 5 ch, 5 ch turn (6 shells);

Row 2: 1 trip tr [dble tr] into first dc [sc], ⋆3 dc [sc] into next lp, 2 ch, 1 dc [sc] into next lp, 3 ch, a 2 trip tr cl [2 dble tr cl] into next 2 ch lp; rep from ⋆ working last cl into last dc [sc], 1 ch, turn.

Rep rows 1 and 2, 9 times more, then rows 2-6 again (10 shell repeats). Fasten off. Slipstitch seams together.

Front edging

Row 1: With wrong side of work facing, attach thread to the base of the last dc [sc] made on row 1, 1 dc [sc] into same place as before, 2 ch, 3 tr [dc] into next sp, ⋆into next sp work 1 dc [sc] 2 ch and 3 tr [dc]; rep from ⋆ along front edge ending with 1 dc [sc] into base of last dc [sc], do not fasten off.

Lower edging
(continuing with working thread)

Row 1: Work 25 dc [sc] evenly along row-ends of main section to

seam, 1 dc [sc] into seam, 22 dc [sc] along back panel to next seam, 1 dc [sc] into seam, 25 dc [sc] along row ends of main section working last dc [sc] into same place as first st on front edging, 3 ch, turn;

Row 2: Miss 1st dc [sc], 1 tr [dc] into next dc [sc], ⋆3 ch, miss 2 dc [sc], 1 tr [dc] into each of next 2 dc [sc]; rep from ⋆ ending with 1 ch, turn;

Row 3: 1 dc [sc] into 1st tr [dc], 1 dc [sc] between last and next tr [dc], ⋆3 dc [sc] into next lp, 1 dc [sc] between next 2 sts; rep from ⋆ ending with 1 dc [sc] into 3rd of 3 ch, 1 ch, turn;

Row 4: 1 dc [sc] into each dc [sc]. Fasten off.

Finishing: Using a damp cloth and hot iron, gently press the bonnet into shape. Press the double-faced satin ribbon and thread it carefully through the holes of lower edging.

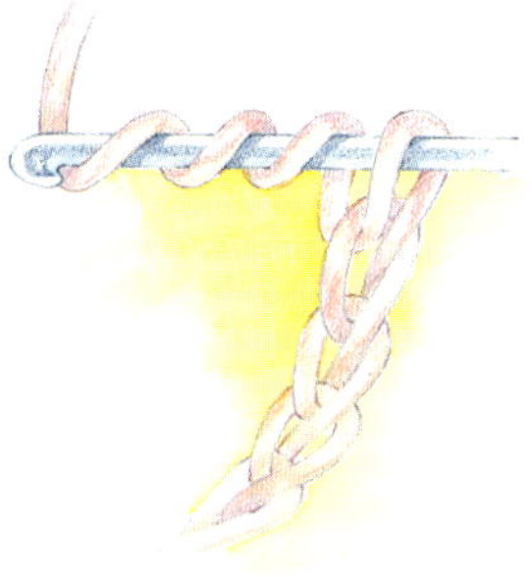

Triple treble (double treble)

White Jointed Mohair Teddy

This delightful bear should be well within the reach of most needleworkers who have a working knowledge of soft-toy or dressmaking techniques. His eyes and joints conform to current safety regulations so he would be the perfect gift for a newly born baby boy or girl, and sure to take pride of place in the nursery.

MATERIALS

soft and hard lead pencils
tracing paper
thin card
craft scissors
non-smudge pen
0.25m (¼yd) mohair in ivory
1 reel of basting cotton in ivory
15cm (6in) square of tussah silk in ivory
1 reel all-purpose sewing cotton in ivory
tailor's chalk in yellow
wooden spoon or piece of dowelling (for stuffing)
selection of needles
one 60mm plastic safety joint, for neck
four 50mm plastic safety joints, for limbs
1 reel of heavy duty nylon thread in white
1 kilo (2¼lb) polyester toy filling
two 15mm amber and black safety locking eyes
1 skein of medium-weight embroidery silk (floss) in terracotta
soft bristled brush

MEASUREMENTS
Height: 50cm (20in)

1 Using a photocopier with a 200% enlarging facility, photocopy the pattern on pages 118 and 119. Trace over the outlines of all pattern shapes and transfer these to thin card. Using a non-smudge pen, transfer all pattern markings. Carefully cut round each template.

2 Lay the fabric face down on a flat surface so that the pile runs towards you. Mark several large arrows using tailor's chalk to denote the direction of the pile and, matching these to the arrows on the templates, draw around each the required number of times, flipping over the template where necessary. Cut out pattern pieces, using sharp, pointed scissors and being careful not to damage the fur pile. Cut pads and paws from silk.

3 Pin, baste and machine stitch the leg, body and ear sections together, the paws to inner-arm sections, and the lower muzzle seam, leaving open between the notches where appropriate for stuffing. Insert the centre-head gusset between the two side-head sections, easing a little if necessary to pin in place. Baste and machine stitch centre-head gusset to side-head

sections. Pin, baste and machine stitch inner and outer arms. Pin and baste footpads into lower feet, and machine stitch in place. Turn all sections right sides out and then gently tease any trapped pile from stitching.

4 Push the shank of each safety eye through the fur fabric at the placement position, cutting a few strands of fabric, if necessary. Using a cotton reel, push the holding washer into position securely.

Firmly stuff the head section, packing the polyester filling well by using the stuffing stick. When stuffing is completed, run a line of basting stitches around the neck opening, leaving the needle and thread attached. Assemble the first part of the largest safety joint, by threading a washer and disc on to the plastic mushroom. Insert the head of the joint into the neck opening and pull the basting thread up tightly to enclose. Run a few extra basting stitches back and forth across the

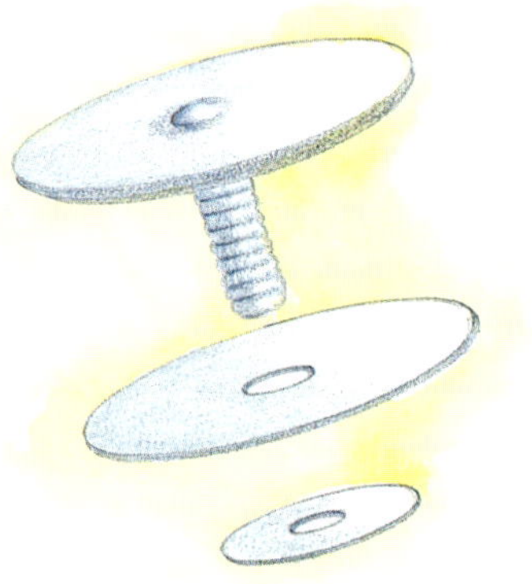

Threading washer and locking disc onto the shank

The first teddy bear was made in New York, by a Russian immigrant storekeeper, Morris Michtom, and his wife, Rose. Morris had been inspired to create a new type of toy, by the now famous cartoon which appeared in the Washington Evening Post. This cartoon told the story of President Theodore Roosevelt who, while out on a bear hunt, refused to shoot the little cub brought to him by eager followers. The sentiment gripped the American nation's imagination, and the Michtoms were soon writing to the President to ask permission to call their innovation 'Teddy's bear'. Permission was granted and the teddy bear was launched on the world. An affectionate childhood companion for many people, Teddy continues to prove one of the most popular toys around, providing love and comfort in his own special way.

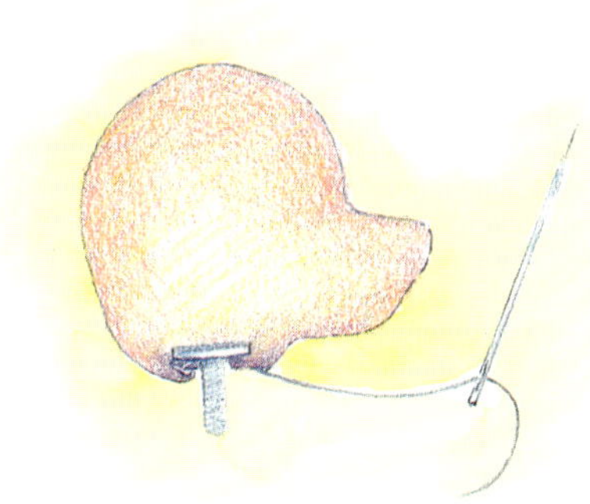

Inserting joint into the neck

opening before finishing off with a few oversewing stitches.

5 Turn in a small seam allowance on each ear and sew these in position using heavy nylon thread and small oversewing stitches. Pull up the thread tightly before finishing with a few small oversewing stitches. Embroider the nose and mouth using silk thread.

6 Using a knitting needle or stiletto, gently prise apart the upper body seam stitching in the correct position for the neck joint. Push through the shank of the joint and secure by threading on the second disc and holding washer. Push down with the cotton reel.

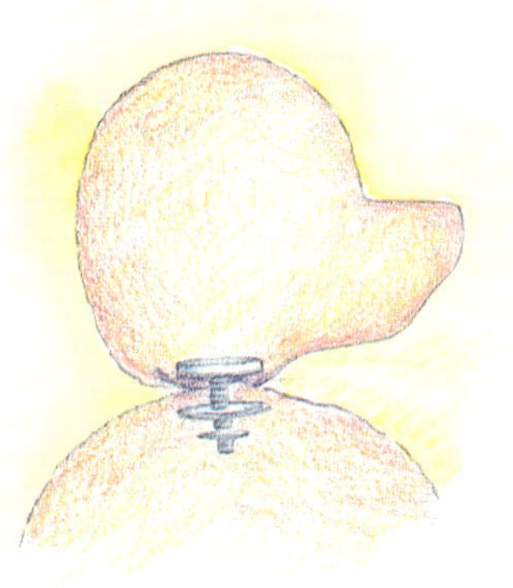

Securing the second disc

7 Firmly stuff the limbs, inserting the head of each safety joint in the correct position. Once stuffed, close all seams by ladderstitching. Attach limbs to the body at the correct placement points, being sure to check that the arms and feet are facing forwards before closing the joints.

8 Stuff the body firmly and ladderstitch back opening. Lightly brush bear using a soft bristled brush.

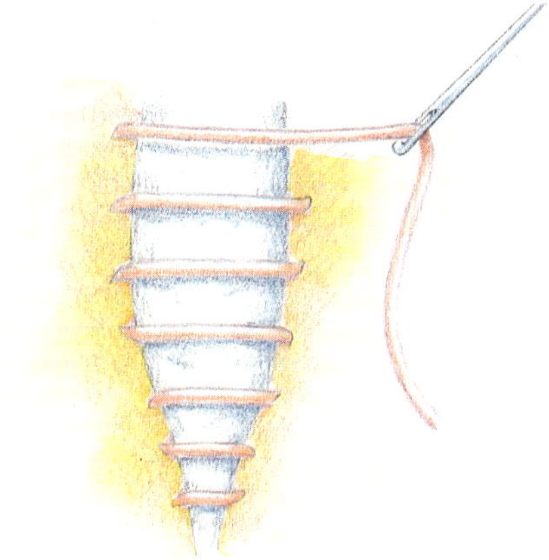

Ladder stitch

Fine Lawn Christening Robe

This fine robe requires a good knowledge of dressmaking, and access to a sewing machine with a swing needle. Although the skills required are not exceptional, working on such fine fabric and in such tiny detail does require a certain amount of confidence and dexterity. Pin tucks must be accurately worked to enable the yoke and front panel to fit correctly. Many of the steps have been worked by hand to give an extra quality to this garment, adding to the definite feel of a treasured classic. You might well further personalise this gift, by adding your initials along the lower back hemline, together with a distinctive mark, such as a rosebud or tiny bird, worked in white silks.

MATERIALS

soft lead pencil
2.25m (2½yd) of 90cm (36in)-wide fine cotton lawn in white
0.75m (30in) of 40mm (1½in)-wide cotton lace insertion in white
5.5m (6yd) of 12mm (2in)-wide white lace
0.75m (30in) of 6mm (¼in)-wide white single-faced satin ribbon
2m (2yd) of thin cord
6 tiny pearl buttons

1 Using a photocopier, enlarge the patterns given on page 116 for the front side panel and side back. Enlarge by 370% and use several sheets of paper for each pattern piece if necessary. Cut out the pattern shapes carefully, reassemble as necessary and mark with the pattern markings.

2 Press the fabric flat and draw a warp and weft thread to find the straight grain. Always cut pattern pieces on the straight grain. Measure and cut a long rectangle 75 x 18cm (30 x 7in) for the front panel; a 22.5cm (9in) square for the yoke; two rectangles measuring 5 x 50cm (2 x 20in) for the waist ties and a strip measuring 7.5 x 50cm (3 x 20in) for the front hem frill.

3 Place the selvage edges of the remaining fabric together and, pinning the paper pattern in place, cut out two front side panels and two side back pieces. From the remaining fabric cut a neck binding strip on the bias of the material. This should measure 2.5 x 25cm (1 x 10in).

4 Following the diagram, and referring to the photograph make tucks, insert lace and attach ribbon onto the front panel. Insert lace by cutting the fabric and attaching the lace using zig-zag stitch. When inserts are completed, carefully trim fabric away behind the lace, close to the stitching lines.

5 Gather one edge of the front hem frill to fit the lower edge of the front panel and stitch together, right sides facing. Run a line of gathering stitches along the upper edge of the front panel. Do not pull the gathering stitches up at this stage.

6 Make pin tucks on the yoke section as shown in the diagram.

7 Fold waist ties over, right sides together, and baste along one short and one long edge. Machine stitch, remove basting stitches, clip corners and turn right side out. Press lightly.

8 Insert front panel between two front side panels, right sides facing, baste and machine stitch seams. Remove basting stitches.

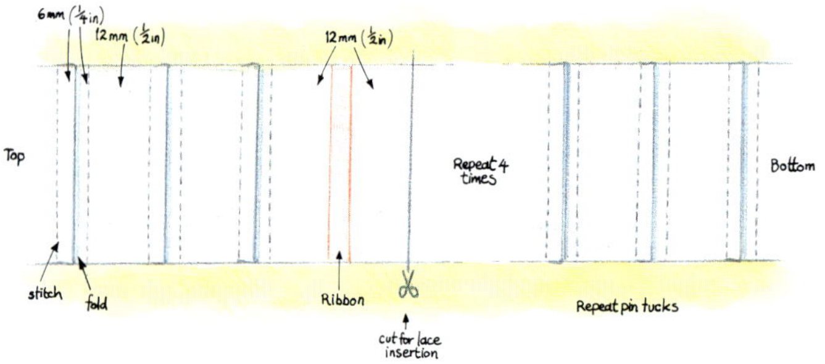

Positioning tucks, inset lace and ribbon on the front panel

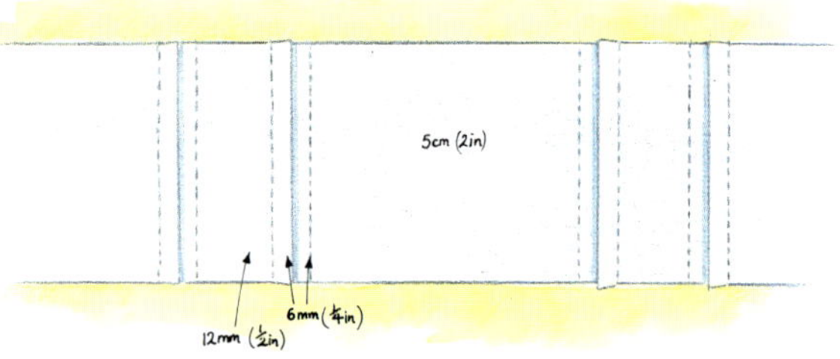

Positioning tucks on the yoke

9 Pin together at the shoulders the front section and the two side back pieces, right sides facing. Baste and machine stitch seams. Remove basting stitches and press lightly.

10 Gather inner shoulder edges and back sections between the notches and pin in place to fit the yoke.

11 Place waist ties in position at upper outer corners of the front panel, gather top edge of front panel to fit yoke and, with right sides together, stitch yoke in position.

12 Gather in narrow lace and stitch in place around front panel and around yoke.

13 Turn in a 6mm (1/4in) double hem on centre-back edges of robe and stitch using herringbone stitch.

14 Turn up a 6mm (1/4in) hem along lower edge of robe, press and stitch on narrow lace trim.

15 Cut out an oval neck opening, measuring 17.5cm (7in) all round and bind with neck binding, leaving ends open. Thread thin cord through binding for fastening neck.

16 Turn up a tiny hem on each sleeve, and make eyelets through which thin cord can be threaded. Edge each sleeve with lace. Thread in thin cord, draw up the sleeve cuff and tie the cord in a bow.

17 Make small buttonhole loops at 6cm (2½in) intervals down one side of centre back hem, and sew on buttons opposite. Press robe lightly.

In the 18th century, lace christening robes such as this would have been a luxury, available only to the rich and powerful. Before the advent of the Leaver's lace machines during the 19th century Industrial revolution, the making of lace would have been a time consuming and skilled occupation. The noble ladies who commissioned the lace would have had little knowledge of the lives of the women who made such wonderful fabrics. Their only desire was to show their wealth and influence by wearing lace with the maximum impact. Often such families passed down their garments from generation to generation, removing and preserving the lace, when eventually the linen it decorated had deteriorated. We must thank the engineers and inventors of the last century for bringing the luxury of lace to us all and for enabling us to create our own heirloom robes to be handed down through our families.

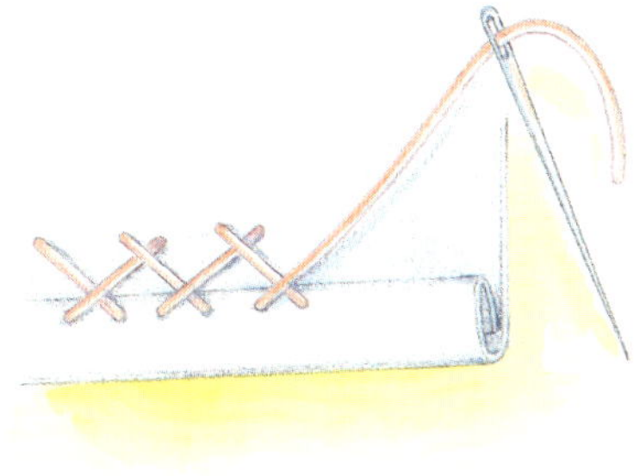

Herringbone stitch

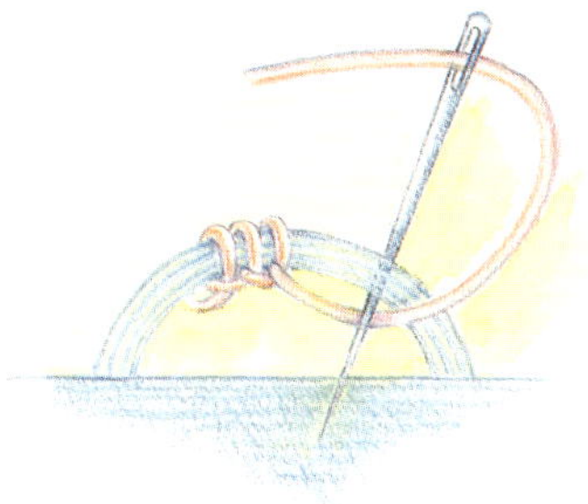

Making buttonhole loops

Baby's First Birthday

Baby's first birthday is a very special event, which cries out to be marked by the gift of something to treasure. In the projects, patchwork, needlepoint and appliqué have been chosen to honour and delight an important and much loved member of the family.

Patchwork Photograph Album Cover

Every fond family loves to collect photographs of their infant's development and what better time to gather those memories together in a very special photograph album than baby's first birthday. This pretty patchwork album cover is made in the traditional way over papers using precious scraps of fabric. Your own choice of colours and patterns will open up a wealth of possibilities.

MATERIALS

photograph album
calico 25mm (1in) larger all round than album
lightweight wadding (batting), 25mm (1in) larger all round album
plain cotton fabric, 25mm (1in) larger all round than album, plus an equal amount for inner sleeves
scraps of light and dark cotton, patterned or plain
soft pencil
thick paper or thin card
pins
'sharps' needle
all-purpose sewing thread
sharp scissors
fine cord or braid (optional)
tracing paper

1 Open photograph album out flat. Measure the height and total width of the open album, including an allowance for the spine. Cut one rectangle each of calico, wadding (batting) and plain cotton for the lining, 25mm (1in) larger than the album.

2 Trace around the larger template shown on page 119 and mark out the shape on the wrong side of one of the fabric scraps, using a soft pencil. Cut out enough fabric shapes from the light and dark fabrics to cover the album. Trace around the smaller template and cut the same number of patches from paper or card.

3 Place one paper shape in the centre of one of the fabric shapes on the wrong side of the fabric, and pin. Fold the seam allowance over the paper, making sure that the fold lies tight against the paper. Baste all around the shape, through the two layers of fabric and the paper. Repeat the process for all the fabric and paper pieces.

Cross Stitch Nursery Picture

Favourite toys provide us with some of our most enduring childhood memories. Here a well loved teddy and floppy rag doll share the nursery shelf; the bear's worn fur and doll's patched pinny are testimony to many years of cuddles. Soft, antique shades have been chosen by the designer Sue Cook to give this cross stitch project the look of an old story book illustration. Simple embroidery stitches have been incorporated to add interest and texture, while the tassels on the faded patchwork quilt give an extra dimension. Finally, to give a special heirloom feeling, tiny golden charms have been stitched on to make this picture a perfect gift to be treasured by a new generation. Note that Aida fabric is not recommended for this project because of the fractional and embroidery stitches used.

MATERIALS

40 x 45cm (16 x 18in) 27/28-count 'Linda' even weave fabric in antique ivory
DMC stranded cotton (floss) as shown in the chart key
Kreinik Braid 02 in metallic gold for drum stringing and bow attaching large heart charm to shelf
Madeira 'Glissengloss' Sterling metallic blending thread in shade 07 gold (to mix with stranded cotton [floss] as shown on the chart key)
DMC 801 (Anchor 0359) for doll's hair embroidery (not listed in key)
Small golden charms (optional)

MEASUREMENTS

Stitch count: 104 high x 130 wide
Finished size: approx 19 x 24cm (7½ x 9½in)

1 Find the centre of the fabric by counting threads and the centre of the chart by counting squares. Start stitching from this point. Work all the cross stitch following the chart, using two strands throughout, with the following exceptions. Use one thread for the striped background, and for the shading below the shelf. Mix two strands of Glissengloss metallic blending thread with one strand of stranded cotton (floss) for the areas indicated on the chart.

2 Next, complete all the back stitch outlining in one strand of DMC 838, with the following exceptions. For the stringing on the drum and the bow attaching the heart charm to the shelf, use Kreinik Braid 02. For the strands of straw on the crown of the doll's hat, use two strands DMC 680. For the bear's nose and muzzle detail, use two strands of black. For the doll's mouth, use two strands of DMC 356. Outline the doll's shoes and all four eyes in one strand of black. (Add one small stitch of white in

the centre of the doll's eyes.) For the stitches in the green quilt squares and the doll's pinafore patch use two strands of DMC 838.

3 When all the cross stitch and back stitch is complete, add the embroidered details. Fill in the bear's inner ear using satin stitch in three strands of DMC 801.

4 Referring to the chart and colour picture, fill in the doll's hair using four strands of DMC 801 and a split straight stitch – the needle piercing each preceding stitch, as in crewel work. Add highlights in the direction shown on the chart, using four strands of DMC 434. NB: If preferred, the doll's hair can be stitched in cross stitch using three strands of the above colours to give a slightly raised effect.

5 Referring to the chart and colour picture, use lazy daisy stitch or detached chain stitch and white thread to make the petals of the flowers. Then stitch French knots in DMC 725 to make the centres, and stitch the leaves and stems in straight stitch in DMC 471.

6 Make each tassel separately, using four mixed strands of DMC 761 and 928, following the dots on the chart, and starting on the outside corner of the quilt. Take the needle and thread through from the front to the back of the fabric, leaving a 2.5cm (1in) tail on the front. Bring the needle through to the front alongside the tail and tie a knot. Trim to the required length and smooth flat.

7 Attach the charms, if using them, using the colour picture as a guide.

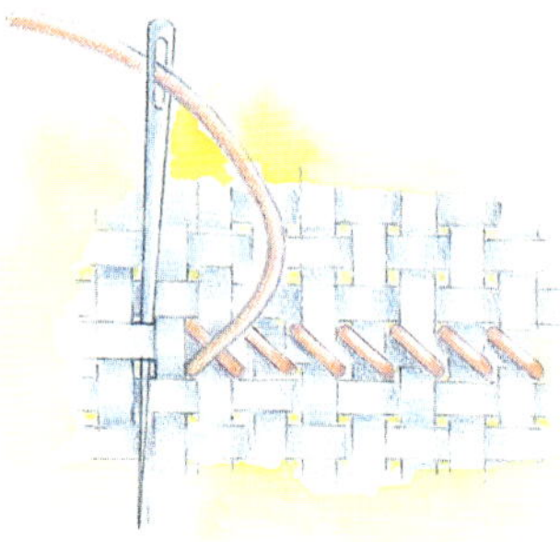

Cross stitch (a)

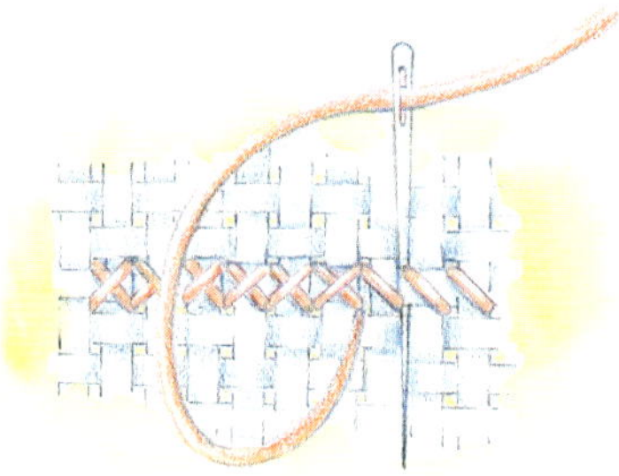

Cross stitch (b)

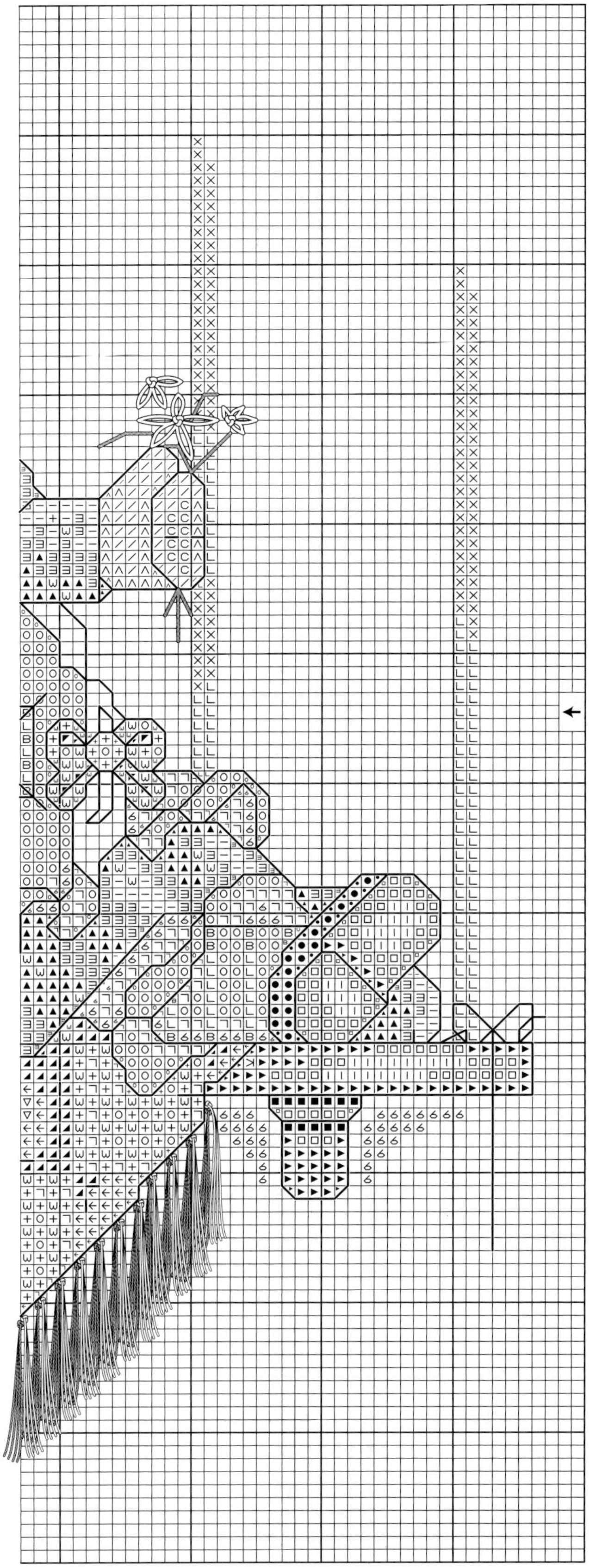

KEY

DMC stranded cotton (floss)

■	White	000
▶	Dark lavender	209
□	Medium lavender	210
|	Light lavender	211
◢	Black	310
←	Medium-dark coral	350
▽	Dark terracotta	355
⬟	Medium Terracotta	356
B	Medium brown	433
L	Light brown	434
C	Very light brown	435
◤	Tan	436
\\\\	Light tan	437
X	Light avocado green	471
=	Medium-light beige grey	644
↓	Light old gold	676
//	Very light old gold	677
I	Dark old gold	680
O	Medium topaz	725
▲	Medium old gold	729
Ǝ	Very light tan	738
—	Light peach flesh	754
●	Light terracotta	758
A	Medium-light salmon	760
K	Light salmon	761
▪▪	Light beige grey	822
4	Very dark beige brown	838
▬	Dark beige brown	839
Y	Medium beige brown	840
S	Light beige brown	841
1	Medium-dark grey blue	926
△	Medium grey blue	927
6	Light grey blue	928
\\	Medium-dark antique blue	930
N	Medium antique blue	931
9	Medium-light antique blue	932
⊥	Very light peach flesh	948
◸	Medium-dark salmon	3328
◇	Medium salmon	3712
/	Light antique blue	3753
Λ	Medium-dark terracotta	3830
W	1 x DMC 676 plus 2 x Glissengloss 07	
+	1 x DMC 677 plus 2 x Glissengloss 07	
⌝	1 x DMC 729 plus 2 x Glissengloss 07	

Drum strings: Kreinik Braid 02

Doll's hair: DMC 801

Embroidered and Appliquéd Hobby Horse

This charming hobby horse is based on a design that has been popular with children for centuries. His tousled mane is simply made from good quality cotton fringing and his wooden body from a broom handle. The woodwork involved is well within the capabilities of any craftsperson and has been specially designed to be both sturdy and decorative. This horse's head has been worked in heavy quality slubbed silk, but a linen union or upholsery velvet cold be substituted. When making this horse for a very small child, omit the bells entirely as a safety precaution.

MATERIALS

HB pencil
craft scissors
dressmaker's scissors
dressmaker's pins
0.5m (½yd) of 90cm (36in)-wide slub silk or woollen tweed medium weight fabric
2m (2yd) of 40mm (1½in)-wide cotton braid with long fringe, in toning colour, for mane
two 18mm safety locking eyes
all-purpose cotton thread in matching shade
1 skein black embroidery silk
large-eyed embroidery needle
500g of hygienic and fire-retardant polyester filling suitable for children's toys
0.5m (½yd) of decorative braid for nose band
1m (1yd) of narrow braid in red or toning colour for reins
4 or 6 braid tassels (optional)
6 large bells
broom handle cut to 1m (36in)
30cm (12in) of wooden dowelling
circular cutter
25mm (1in) panel pin
15cm (6in) square of soft wood, measuring 5cm (2in) thick
all-purpose extra strong adhesive
sandpaper
beeswax polish

1 Using a photocopier, enlarge the pattern pieces given on page 117. Enlarge them by 200% and divide each pattern piece onto several sheets of paper is necessary. Cut out the pattern shapes carefully. Reassemble them as necessary and mark with the pattern markings.

2 Pin the pattern pieces to the silk fabric, making sure that the grain lines indicated on the pattern are running in the correct direction.

3 Cut out the pattern pieces as directed on the pattern.

4 Place the two side-head sections right sides together and baste from above the eye position, around the end of the muzzle to the neck (leaving neck open). Machine stitch this seam.

5 Slash the fabric along the lines marked for placing the ears and set head aside.

6 Place each pair of ear pieces right sides together. Pin, baste and machine stitch, leaving the lower edges open. Remove basting stitches, and turn right sides out.

7 Fold the end of each ear as shown in the diagram and tuck into cut holes in side-head sections, making sure to turn in a tiny seam allowance on each side of the holes. Turn head inside out and baste ears in position. Machine stitch and remove basting stitches.

Folding the ear

8 Starting from the back of the neck, pin one side of the head gusset to one of the side-head pieces, right sides together, tapering the seam into the point where the two side-head pieces join. Baste and remove pins. Pin the second side in position, pin and baste. Machine stitch and remove basting stitches. If any gap remains between the gusset seams and muzzle seam, machine stitch this closed. Turn head right sides out.

9 Insert the eyes in the position marked, following the instructions given for the teddy bear on page 18. Made sure that they are firmly secured before proceeding to the next step.

10 Stuff the head firmly, making sure that the machined ends of the ears face downwards. This will ensure that the ears stand upright. Once the head is firmly stuffed, oversew the lower neck seam using strong thread, leaving sufficient space to insert the end of the broom handle. Positon it towards the back of the neck and push it up to the top of the head.

11 Cut two lengths of fringed braid long enough to run from the back of the neck to the point of the gusset (between the ears) and back again. Stitch these lengths of braid in position, one on top of the other, to form a mane (fold them into a point between the eyes).

12 Cut a length from the remaining fringed braid, long enough to run around the lower neck edge. Stitch this in position using tiny oversewing stitches.

13 Cut a sufficient length of the decorative braid to make a strap around the muzzle, and stitch this securely in place.

14 Stitch the bells firmly to the narrow braid at intervals and stitch this to the head to form reins. A few tassels can be sewn in place if desired, using matching heavy-duty thread and oversewing stitches.

15 Embroider the nostrils using black embroidery thread and bullion stitch. The mouth is suggested with four strands of embroidery thread straight stitched across the lower muzzle.

16 Cut the broom handle to a length of 97cm (38in) and

In the early 18th century, playthings for children were not in great demand. Children were, at that time, encouraged to be miniature adults, in a way that we would find disturbing today. However, crudely made items that mimicked the life of a grown-up could be bought at fairs and from the pedlars who called around the villages from time to time. One of the most popular items, whether roughly carved from a plank of wood, or pieced together from scraps of material, was the hobby horse, designed to enable a young child to grasp the notion of horse riding. Indeed, the first hobby horses were made of wicker and were hung from the waists of morris dancers, whose actions resembled those of a capering horse. The first hobby horse made as a child's toy appeared as early as 1589.

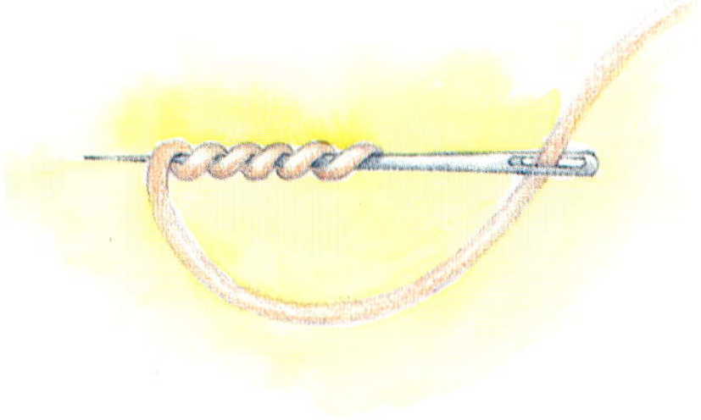

Bullion stitch (a)

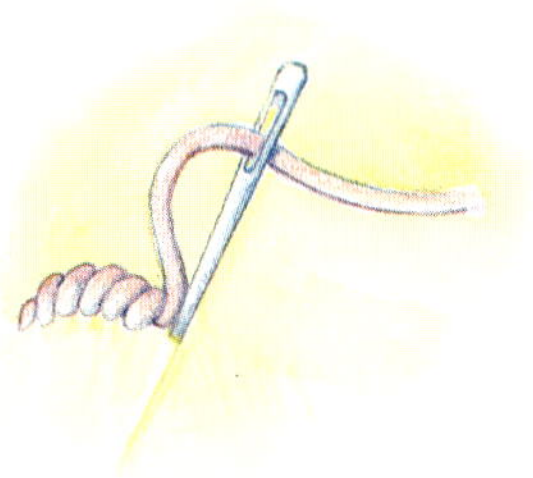

Bullion stitch (b)

sandpaper the cut edge smooth. Drill two holes through the broom handle large enough to take the dowelling comfortably. The first hole should be 36cm (14in) from the cut edge and the second 4cm (1½in) from the shaped end. The holes should be slightly larger than the diameter of the dowelling to enable this to move freely when the wheels are attached. Using a hacksaw cut one piece of dowelling approximately 33cm (13in) and the other 7cm (2¾in). Push the longer piece through the first hole, so that it is central. Hold this in place with a panel pin, which is hammered through the broom handle and into the dowelling.

17 Using a circular cutter, cut 2 circles of wood from the soft wood square for the wheels. Each circle should measure 5cm (2in). Drill a hole through the centre of each, slightly larger than the diameter of the dowelling. Insert the remaining length of dowelling through the second hole in the broom handle and attach a wheel at either end. Glue in place with a little wood glue. Leave to dry until completely set. The dowelling should move freely within the handle, so that the wheels can turn. Finish by sandpapering lightly to remove any rough edges and seal by polishing with a good quality beeswax polish.

18 Push the cut edge of the broom handle into position within the head and glue to fabric opening for extra strength. Make sure neck is stitched tightly closed either side of the broom handle. Leave to dry thoroughly before use.

126
127
128
129
130
131
132
107
108
109
110

First Home Together

When a couple set up home for the first time, it is a pleasure to mark the occasion with a personalised gift which expresses good wishes and love for their future happiness together. In this chapter, simple cross-stitch, patchwork and drawn-thread work have been used to provide mementoes which can be used and appreciated for the years to come.

MONOGRAMMED AND CROSS-STITCHED TOWELS

These dainty velvet-pile fingertip towels would provide a thoughtful and welcome gift for a couple setting up home together. Easy and quick to work in cross-stitch, they make a decorative and personal addition to any bathroom, and will blend well with many styles of interior decoration. There are several towel shades and the colours of the threads could be varied to give different colourways. The designs could also be embroidered on bathrobes and bed linen, using the waste-canvas technique.

MATERIALS

Charles Craft luxury fingertip towels with Aida band: one each of pink and white
graph paper
HB pencil
30cm (12in) embroidery hoop
basting cotton in contrasting colour
no. 8 tapestry needle
embroidery scissors

Anchor stranded cotton (floss) one skein each, as listed in the key

1 Place the towel into an embroidery hoop so that the Aida band is central.

2 Choose the required initials from the chart on page 43 and chart these on to graph paper. The width of letters varies slightly, so you may wish to chart out the whole design (see page 43) on both sides of the lettering, to ensure that you have sufficient width on the towel. If in any doubt, place the stems of the flowers closer together under the letter. Once you are happy with the balance of your design, count to the centre of the Aida band and mark this with a basting stitch.

3 Following your chart, embroider the initial and the floral design, using the colour key provided on page 43. As the back of the work will be visible when completed, make sure to fasten in the tails of thread as you work. Run the needle behind a few stitches when starting and finishing to make the thread secure.

VIOLETTE
M
R

4 When the work is completed, neaten any remaining tails of thread and press the design lightly on the wrong side onto a soft towel.

5 Complete the second towel in the same manner. When washing the towels, follow the manufacturer's instructions.

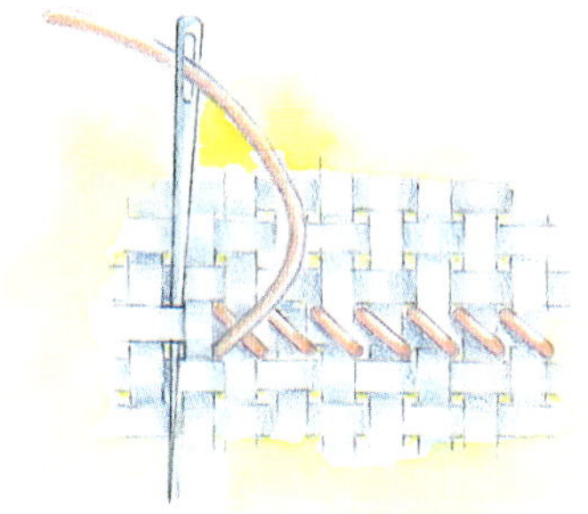

Cross stitch (a)

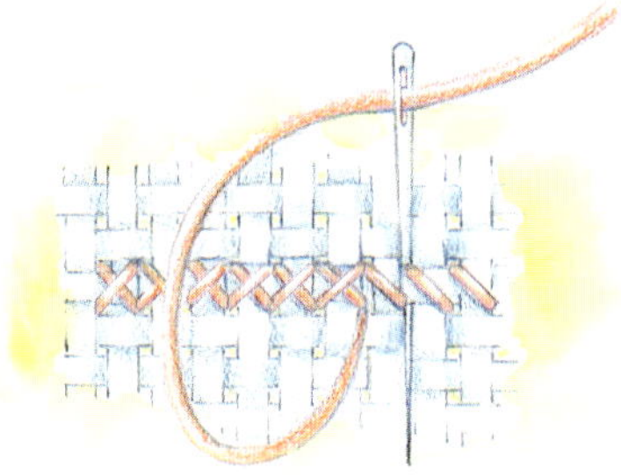

Cross stitch (b)

Monogrammed and embroidered linen has always been popular. In the large households of previous centuries, it was a decorative necessity for identification, as the weekly or monthly wash would combine the linen of many individuals. As time went on the decorative element of embroidered monograms remained popular, and in Victorian times many ornate styles and techniques were developed.

KEY

Anchor stranded cotton (floss)

●	901	caramel
▼	868	dusky peach
◸	1041	dark grey/green
↘	39	rose pink
+	305	bright yellow
●	845	leaf green
▼	26	candy pink
◸	128	light sky blue
↘	140	dark sky blue
+	256	light leaf green

CUTWORK CHERRY TABLECLOTH

This pretty set of tablecloth and matching napkins, designed by Jan Eaton, is perfect for a traditionally English afternoon tea. The cutwork cherry motifs are worked in shades of lustrous stranded cotton (floss) to complement the pale-green scalloped border around the edge of both cloth and napkins. Linen is the best fabric to use for cutwork as the fibres are strong enough to bear the strain of supporting the cut-away areas. Here the embroidered areas are strengthened with a layer of embroidery backing to ensure successful laundering. The design could be adapted to fit a larger rectangular cloth by adding extra scallops to the border. The quantities given will make the tablecloth plus six napkins.

MATERIALS

2.3m (2½yd) of 140cm (55in)-wide Zweigart Edinburgh linen in antique white (101)
DMC stranded cotton (floss) in the following colours;
1 skein of white;
2 skeins of red 309;
3 skeins of deep green 320;
11 skeins of pale green 369
2 packs Vilene Stitch 'n' Tear embroidery backing
water-soluble embroidery marker
basting thread
sewing needle
crewel needle no. 7
dressmaker's shears
embroidery scissors
fine pins
tracing paper
HB pencil
fine-point black felt pen with permanent ink
masking tape

MEASUREMENTS

Tablecloth: 126 x 126cm (49½ x 49½in)
Napkins: 35 x 35cm (14 x 14in)

1 Cut off the selvages along the straight grain of the fabric. Withdraw a single thread across the cut ends of the fabric to straighten them and cut off any surplus. Press the fabric with a hot steam iron to remove folds and wrinkles.

2 To cut out the tablecloth, measure 140cm (55in) from one end of the fabric and withdraw a single thread across the fabric. Cut along this line. For the napkins, fold the remaining fabric in half across the width and mark the fold with a pin. Withdraw a thread across the fabric at this mark and cut along the line, giving you two identical strips of fabric. Fold each strip across the width to give three equal portions. Mark, draw a thread along each fold and cut into pieces as before.

3 For the tablecloth, trace off the triple scalloped shape on page 46 six times, on separate pieces of tracing paper using the pencil. Trace off the circular shape containing the cherry motif twice in the same way. Draw over the pencil

TABLECLOTH DESIGN

NAPKIN DESIGN

KEY

DMC stranded cotton (floss)

Cut-away areas		░
Cherries	**red**	**309**
Leaves and stalks	**deep green**	**320**
Border and roundels	**pale green**	**369**
Highlights-white french knots		**blanc**
Leaf veins-deep green stem stitch		**320**

lines with the black felt pen to strengthen them. Carefully join the scallop tracings together along the dotted lines until you have a straight line of eighteen scallops. Join one end piece to each end of the row of scallops.

4 Lay the tracing on a large, flat surface and secure it with several strips of masking tape. Position one edge of the tablecloth evenly over the top of the tracing, with the fabric edge about 4cm (1½ in) beyond the lower edge of the scallop pattern. Secure the fabric with strips of masking tape set at right angles across the raw edge.

5 Trace the solid lines of the design on to the fabric with the water-soluble marker. Mark the areas to be cut away on the cherry motifs (see pattern). Peel off the masking tape and position the second (adjoining) edge of the tablecloth over the tracing, aligning the circular end sections. Trace the design, then repeat steps 4 and 5 until the design has been transferred to all sides of the tablecloth.

6 For the napkins, trace off the napkin design on page 46 as follows: once with the scalloped edge and the circular shape and three times with only the scalloped edge. Join the four tracings together along the dotted lines to make a square design. Transfer the design on to each of the six smaller squares of fabric in the same way as for the tablecloth. Do not press the fabric once the water-soluble marker has been applied, as the heat of the iron will fix the ink permanently to the fabric.

7 Cut the embroidery backing into 8cm (3in) deep strips. Position the strips on the wrong side of the fabric, centring each piece over a portion of the design, and pin in place. You will need to use several strips of backing to cover the scalloped edge and corner motifs, so overlap the pieces by about 5mm (¼in). Baste around the edge of each piece of backing, then work two rows of running stitch to outline both inner and outer edges of the scallops. Work several crossing rows of running stitch right across the corner motifs.

8 To stitch the scalloped edges, work two rows of running stitch just inside both inner and outer edges of the scallops with three strands of pale-green thread. Then work buttonhole stitch along the double traced outlines, covering the running stitch lines and making sure that the looped edge of the stitch faces the outside of the scallops. Position the stitches close together so that no background fabric shows through.

9 Work the cherry motifs as follows: work a single line of running stitch using three strands of the appropriate thread colour between the double outlines of the motif. When you reach the position for a bar, strand the thread three times back and forth between the opposite edges. Bring the needle through the fabric just below the strands and work a buttonhole stitch over the strands.

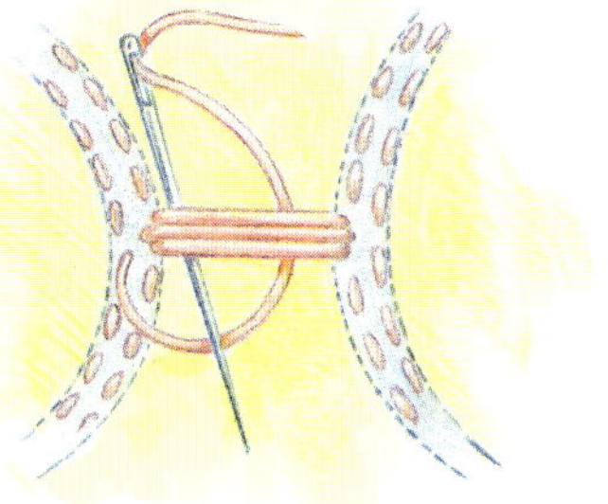

Forming a bar

10 Continue working buttonhole stitch over the strands until you reach the opposite side, working the stitches close together without picking up any fabric with your needle. Take the needle through the fabric between the double outlines and continue working running stitch round the motif

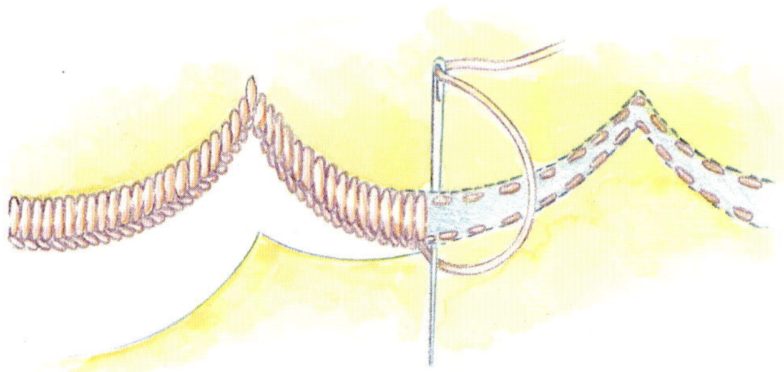

Working the scalloped edges with buttonhole stitch

Cutwork is a European embroidery technique which originated in Flanders and Italy, reaching the height of popularity in England during the 16th and 17th centuries. Traditionally worked in white thread on white linen fabric, cutwork is present in many 17th century English whitework samplers and the technique is considered to be the forerunner of all needle made laces. Cutwork designs are created by outlining motifs with buttonhole stitch, then cutting away portions of the background fabric. There are two types of cutwork: in the first, the motifs are positioned close together so they touch each other and small portions of the background fabric are cut away. In the second type, which is used to make this cherry-patterned tablecloth and matching napkins, the motifs are spaced out to form the design, leaving larger areas of fabric between them. The motifs are joined with buttonhole-stitched bars, then the background fabric is cut away beneath them to create a delicate, lacy design.

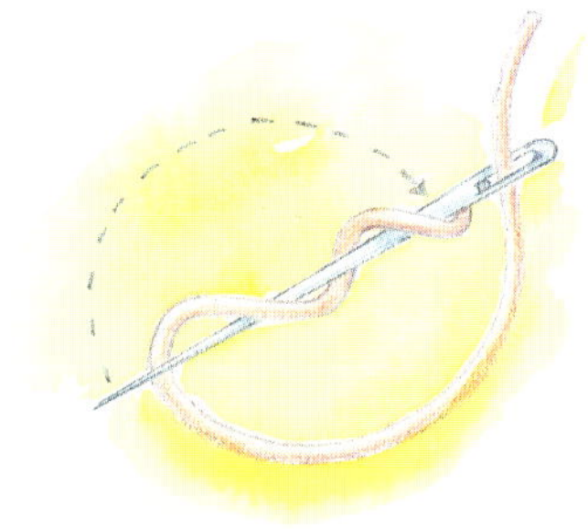

French knot (a)

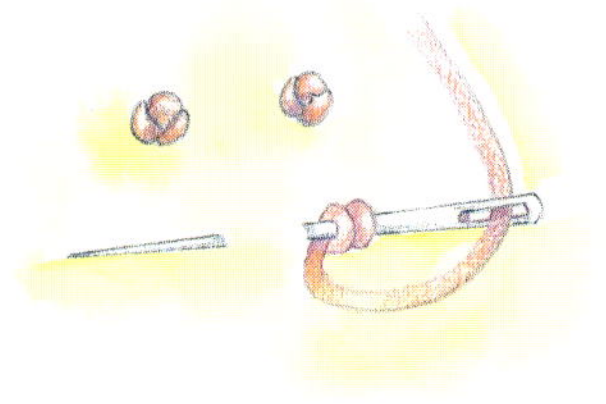

French knot (b)

until the next bar position is reached.

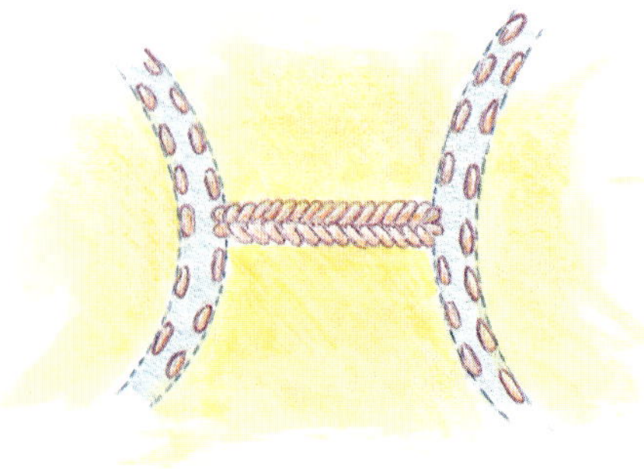

Completed bar

11 Work buttonhole stitch along the double outlines, using three strands of the appropriate colour of thread, covering the running stitch lines and making sure that the looped edge of the stitch faces the areas which are to be cut away. Add the remaining details to the cherry motifs with stem stitch and French knots, again using three strands of the appropriate thread.

12 Remove the tacking stitches, then cut away the marked parts of the motifs using small, sharp scissors. Carefully tear away the backing from round the edges of the motifs and the inner edge of the scallops. To finish the scalloped edge, cut away the outer fabric along the outside edge of the scallops together with the embroidery backing. Use small, sharp scissors and cut as close as you can to the embroidery but take care not to snip into the stitches. Immerse the tablecloth and napkins in cold water to remove the embroidery marker, allow to dry and press with a hot iron.

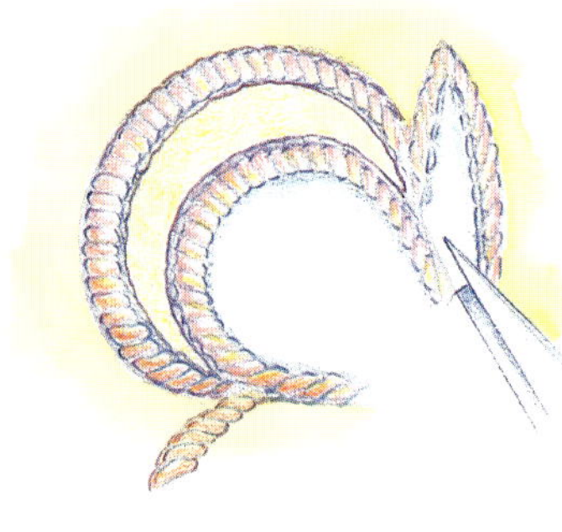

Cutting away the marked parts of the motif

SQUARE DANCE QUILT

An heirloom quilt for a young couple - what could be more fun than starting life together with a family treasure to pass on to future generations. Designed by Christine Porter, this traditional patchwork quilt is relatively easy to make, especially if you already have some quilting experience, and it will fit the top of a double bed. It could also be used as a lap quilt to snuggle under while watching the television, or be hung decoratively over the back of a favourite armchair.

MATERIALS

- approx 0.25m (¼yd) each of minimum 10 red striped fabrics in a wide variety, for the blocks
- approx 0.25m (¼yd) each of minimum 10 blue striped fabrics in a wide variety, for the blocks
- small amount of green striped fabric for the blocks
- 0.5m (½yd) pale-blue-and-white checked fabric for the outer triangles
- 1m (1yd) dark-blue checked fabric for the outer triangles
- 1.75m (1¾yd) dark-blue-and-red checked fabric for the outer border
- 1m (1yd) plain bright-red fabric for the sashing and binding
- 4.5m (4½yd) cotton fabric for the backing
- 204 x 204cm (80 x 80in) wadding (batting)
- rotary cutter, rotary ruler and self-healing mat
- sharps needles
- dressmaker's pins
- small scissors
- medium-blue and red thread for piecing the top
- safety pins or quilt tack gun for machine quilting
- invisible thread for top of machine quilting, plus cotton thread in bobbin, to match backing
- cotton thread for hand quilting
- sewing machine with walking foot for quilting straight lines and darning or embroidery foot for free quilting
- iron and ironing board

MEASUREMENTS

Finished quilt: 180 x180cm (70 x 70in)

100% prewashed cotton is recommended for this quilt, and measurements are based on fabric that is 115cm (45in) wide before washing. The use of rotary cutting equipment helps with accurate cutting. Instructions for cutting are given as you go along - it is best not to cut everything out at the beginning. Note that the instructions for cutting all the pieces include the seam allowance.

1 Sort your fabrics into dark, medium and light groups according to colour. Mix and match each block; the greater the contrast, the more pleasing the design. Lay out each block as you cut it as this offers a chance to let you see the effect before you begin to sew. You may wish to change the colours, keeping 'spares' for the next block. When sewing always use a 5mm (¼in) seam allowance for accuracy.

2 Cut 5 A squares measuring 6.5 x 6.5cm (2½ x 2½in) in light fabric, cut 4 A squares measuring 6.5 x 6.5cm (2½ x 2½in) in dark fabric. Cut 2 squares 13.5 x 13.5cm (5¼ x 5¼ in) in medium fabric, cut

A squares in rows of three

Rows sewn together

Adding B triangles

Adding C triangles

in half on the diagonal to form 4 B triangles. Cut 2 squares 17.5 x 17.5cm (7 x 7in) all in either dark or light fabric, cut in half on the diagonal to form 4 C triangles

3 Sew each block as you cut it, as follows (see diagrams). Sew the A squares together in rows of 3. Press the seams away from the centre in the outside rows, and towards the centre in the middle row. Sew the 3 rows together to make the central square block, pressing the seams open. Sew 2 B triangles to opposite sides of the block, marking the centres of the edges to ensure accurate positioning, pressing the seams towards the triangles. Repeat with the other sides of the block. Add 4 C triangles to the sides of the resulting square, in the same way. Make 13 blocks in the same way.

4 Make the 4 corner blocks in the same way, but with 5 dark and 4 light central squares, and omitting the C triangles.

5 For the outer triangles, cut 4 squares measuring 17.5 x 17.5cm (7 x 7in) in the pale-blue-and-white check. Cut the squares in half diagonally to make 8 D triangles. Mark the mid point of each long side. Seam allowances are included.

6 Cut 8 E strips measuring 45 x 11.5cm (17¾ x 4½in). Mark the mid point of each E strip. Seam allowances are included. Join triangle D to strip E as shown in the diagram, matching mid points. Using the cutting ruler as a guide, trim off excess fabric to form triangle F. Make 8 F triangles.

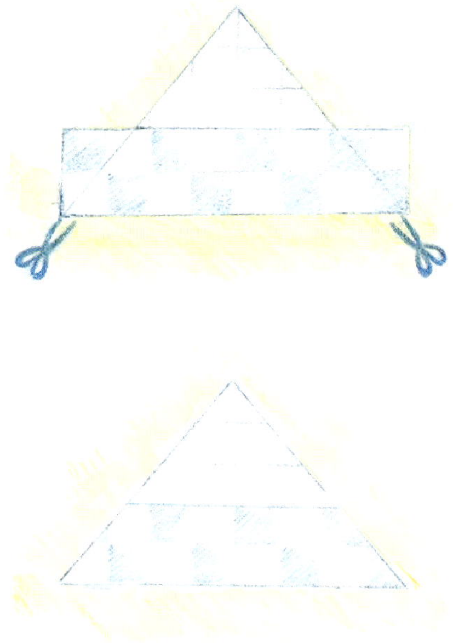

Making triangle F with triangle D and strip E

7 For the corner triangles, cut 2 squares measuring 23.5 x 23.5cm (9¼ x 9¼in) in dark-blue check. Cut them in half diagonally to make 4 G triangles. Seam allowances are included.

8 To assemble the quilt top,refer to the diagram and lay out the 13 large blocks and 8 outer F triangles in diagonal rows, adding the 4 corner triangles (G). Stitch together in diagonal rows, pressing the seams in opposite directions from row to row. Stitch the rows together, pinning the rows carefully to match the seams.

9 For the sashing strip (between the blocks and the outer

border), cut 8 strips measuring 3 x 114cm (1¼ x 45in) in plain bright-red fabric. Join in pairs to make 4 long strips. Measure the quilt top through the centre vertically, and trim 2 strips to this length. Pin the strips in position, matching mid points, then stitch. Measure the quilt top through the centre horizontally, and trim and join the other strips in the same way.

Adding corner blocks to the border strips

10 For the border, cut 4 pieces measuring 23 x 138cm (9 x 48in) in dark-blue-and-red check. Measure the quilt top through the centre vertically and trim the 4 pieces to this length. Matching mid points, pin 2 strips to opposite sides of the quilt top and stitch in place. Attach the corner blocks to each end of the remaining border strips (see diagram), pin in place, matching mid points, and stitch to the quilt top.

Assembling the central design

11 Make a backing piece 8cm (3in) larger all round than the quilt top. Press the seams open. Cut the wadding (batting) to the same size as the backing, and press both pieces. Place together the backing, wadding and quilt top layers, and baste together if hand quilting. If machine quilting, use safety pins or quilt tack gun. Mark the quilting lines of your choice. For the original here the blocks were outline quilted and the outer border was quilted with a clam shell motif, by machine.

12 For the binding, cut 8 strips measuring 6.5 x 138cm

This square dance quilt uses the traditional American nine-patch arrangement, with blocks made up of nine squares. The blocks are positioned to make the 'diamond in the square' pattern which was particularly linked to Lancaster County. but was popular all over America. Often, this type of geometric pattern was used by Amish quilters in order to avoid the intricate designs which were fashionable in the late nineteenth century.

Square Dance quilt

(2½ x 48in), in plain bright-red fabric. Join the strips together to make a continuous strip of fabric. Press wrong sides together lengthwise to make a 3cm (1¼in)-wide double binding. Attach to the quilt, right sides together, mitring the corners, and using a 5mm (¼in) seam allowance. Fold the binding over to the back and sew it in place, tucking in the raw end and stitching down the mitred corners.

WEDDING ROMANCE

When two people decide to declare their love for each other by entering into a marriage contract, it is fitting for those nearest and dearest to the happy couple to offer gifts which reflect the romance and dreams of this special day. A token made with care, with the recipients in mind, is a mark of love and esteem that will be treasured for years. Whether you decide on a lacey garter or a romantic but more practical bed throw, you can be sure that these projects will be appreciated by the new husband and wife alike.

Lace Garter

This garter combines all the good luck requirements of a gift to a new bride – something old, something new, something borrowed and something blue. The use of a garter is indeed an old tradition, and whilst ribbons and lace are new, the motif of antique seed pearls and a pear-shaped crystal 'dropper' provide the touch of 'something old'. The embroidery thread to form the love knots can be 'borrowed' from a friend and, of course, the ribbons and rose are blue. If you are fortunate enough to find some, a scrap of old lace would further enhance this very personal and individual gift. Better still, a lacemaker could make a piece of traditional bobbin lace especially for the bride.

MATERIALS

1m (39in) of 10cm (3½in)-wide white cotton double-edged lace
1m (39in) of 12mm (½in) sheer Offray organza ribbon in light blue
1m (39in) of 9mm (⅜in) Offray jacquard ribbon 'fleur' in 'copen'
all-purpose sewing thread in light blue
all-purpose sewing thread in white
1m (39in) of seam binding in white
40cm (16in) of 12mm (½in)-wide white elastic
safety pin
10 Offray sheer ribbon roses in light blue
2 pearl seed beads (optional)
1 crystal drop (optional)
scrap of pink Anchor stranded cotton (floss) 23
beading needle

1 Run a line of long basting stitches along the centre of the double-edged lace.

2 Place the narrow dark blue ribbon in the centre of the lighter blue organza ribbon and baste in place carefully. Then, using the light blue all-purpose thread, secure the two ribbons together by running a line of tiny oversewing stitches along each edge of the narrow ribbon. Fasten off with a few oversewing stitches.

3 Centre the organza ribbon over the central line of basting stitches on the lace, and baste the two ribbons in place. Using white all-purpose thread, oversew both edges of the ribbon in place on the lace using tiny stitches. Remove any visible basting stitches and press the lace and ribbons lightly.

4 Join the two raw edges of lace together, right sides facing, and pin. Baste and then machine stitch, taking a small seam allowance of approximately 5mm (⅜in). Remove

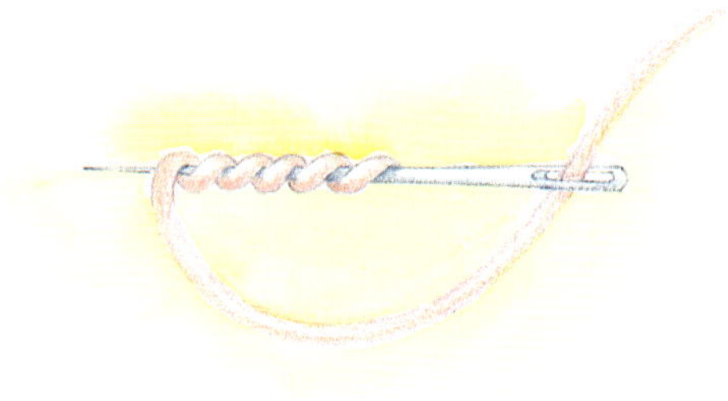

Bullion stitch (a)

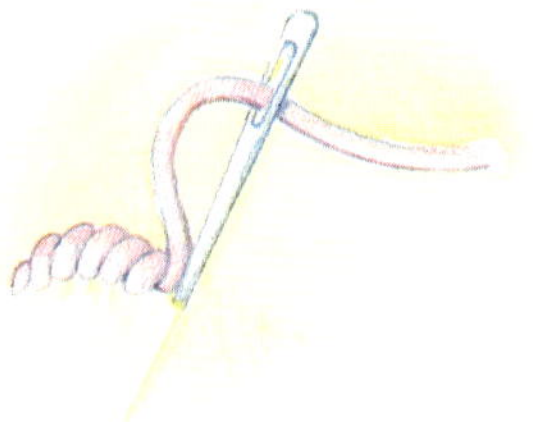

Bullion stitch (b)

basting stitches and neaten by stitching in any loose threads.

5 Using long basting stitches, attach the seam binding tape to the wrong side of the lace, making sure that it will not be visible from the right side. Join to the lace by running a line of tiny oversewing stitches along each edge of the tape and catching up just a little of the lace at each stitch. Leave a little tape unstitched on either side of the machined seam to enable the elastic to be threaded through. Finish off by oversewing securely.

6 Attach a strong safety pin to one side of the elastic tape and thread this through the casing formed on the inside of the garter. As the garter is drawn up, keep moving it along the elastic tape until completely gathered, but making sure that the other end of the elastic remains free. Pin this in place if necessary. Once the garter has been completely gathered to the correct size, use the safety pin to secure both ends of the elastic tape. Cut off any extra elastic tape and join both ends securely together using oversewing stitches.

As far back as the 16th century, garters, which were originally a purely functional means of holding up stockings for both men and women, had, at least for the female sex, taken on a more alluring significance. In the poetry and prose of the time, the interests of the male in this item of feminine apparel had become apparent. The lace garter of the bride was often thrown to the male attendants of the bridegroom, just as the bouquet is still thrown to the bridesmaids. Indeed, at more raucous celebrations, the groom's men were quite likely to take it upon themselves to wrest the garters from the brides and bridesmaids alike.

While not suggesting that we return to these politically incorrect customs, the gift of a garter to a bride is a time-honoured tradition, which is a delight to observe. During times of war, women often carried the initials of their loved ones embroidered on their garters - the more romantic amongst us might be prompted to weave the initials of both bride and groom into the band of blue ribbon before the garter is assembled.

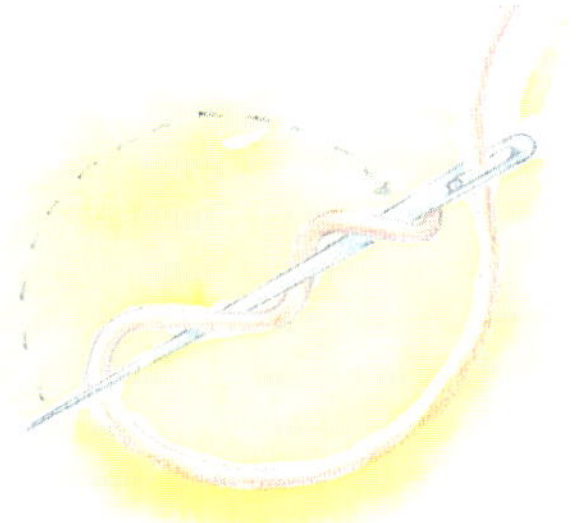

French knot (a)

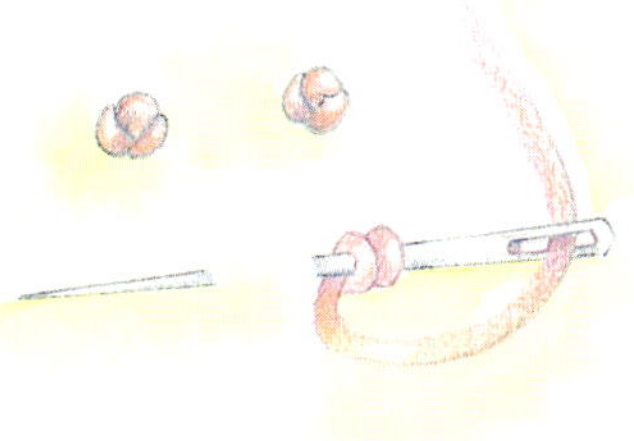

French knot (b)

7 Pull the elastic slightly to settle within the casing tape and, folding in a tiny hem, close the casing tape neatly. Oversew the tape into position and finish off securely.

8 Turn the garter right side out and adjust the gathers. Sew a scattering of sheer ribbon roses in position along the ribbon. At intervals along the lace, add a few pink true-love knots formed from French knots and bullion stitches, in embroidery thread (floss).

9 Finally, using a beading needle, attach a length of all-purpose blue thread to the ribbon band, equidistant from two ribbon roses. Thread on a pearl seed bead, followed by the crystal dropper and the second pearl seed bead. Make a few tiny oversewing stitches a fraction away from the starting position and draw up the thread tightly. Finish with a few more oversewing stitches. Adjust the gathering of the garter and, if necessary, lightly press the lace.

Silk Knitted and Beaded Purse

Few brides would not be charmed to receive a gift such as this beaded purse, to be carried as an individual accessory on that special day. With the continuing appeal of beadwork the purse could then be used as an evening bag for many years to come, or put aside as a family heirloom to be passed from bride to bride. Worked here in white, with iridescent beads, the purse could also be worked in any pale pastels (or even dark, rich colours) to tone with bridal flowers or bridesmaids dresses. Indeed, a purse could be worked for each bridesmaid, to make a lovely memento of a wonderful day.

MATERIALS

1 x 50g (1¾oz) ball of Coats white 'Opera' cotton no. 5 in white
pair 3mm (no. 11) knitting needles
600 x 5mm (¼in) opal glass beads
large-eyed darning needle
small scrap of contrasting yarn
small tub of opal glass bugle beads
small tub of opal glass seed beads
beading needle
one 13cm (5in) handbag frame
25cm (¼yd) silk or linen lining fabric
strong cotton thread

FINISHED SIZE
Width at top of purse: approx 13cm (5in)
Depth including fringing: approx 18cm (7in)

TENSION
8sts and 12 rows to 25mm (1in)

ABBREVIATIONS
k: knit
p: purl
yfwd: yarn forward
b1: yarn forward, slip bead close to work, slip next stitch, yarn back

1 Thread half the large beads onto the yarn using a large-eyed darning needle, which will fit through the hole in the bead.

2 Using this yarn, and 3mm (no. 11) needles, cast on 39 sts loosely. Proceed with beading pattern, as follows:

Row 1: Knit
Row 2 and each alternate row: K1, p to last st, k1
Row 3: K4, *yfwd, slip bead close to work, slip next st, b1, k5, rep from * to last 5 sts, b1, k4
Row 5: K3, *b1, k1, b1, k3, rep from * to end
Row 7: K2, * b1, k3, b1, k1, rep from * to end
Row 9: K1, *b1, k5, rep from * to last 2 sts, k1
Row 10: Purl

These 10 rows form the pattern, which is repeated throughout. Increase one st at each end of row 11 and further 5 rows. Place a small piece of coloured yarn at each end

The turn of the 19th century in England and France saw the heyday of beadwork in the fashion industry. In the French atelier, skilled workers perfected the use of the tambour hook to quickly cover large areas of fabric with a dazzling layer of beads and sequins. Every conceivable combination of beadwork and embroidery was employed to produce the stunning creations of designers such as Paquin and Worth. The little beaded evening purse was an essential accessory for the smart lady-about-town and beads were also combined with knitting and crochet to develop new styles and textures. The combination of seed bead and bugles used on our bridal purse is typical of the 1920s, but is perfect for today's bride who wants to add a personal and feminine touch to her look on this special day.

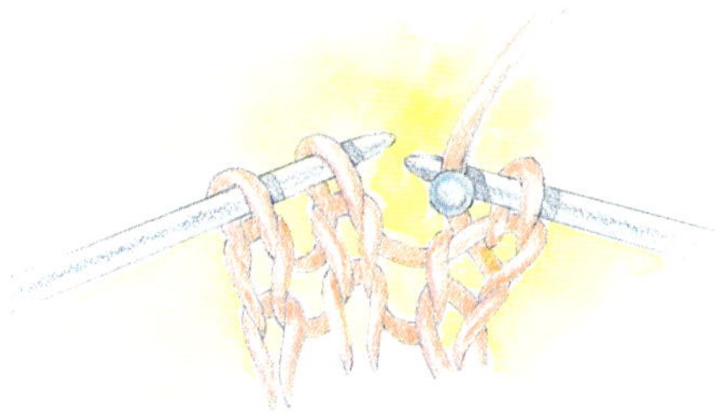

Knitting in the beads (a)

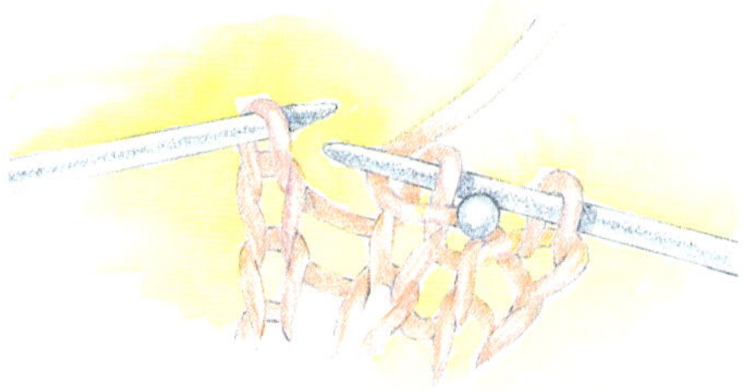

Knitting in the beads (b)

of this row as a sewing marker.
Work 10 rows without shaping.
Decrease 1 st at each end of next and every 4th row until 41 sts remain. Then every alternate row until 33 sts remain. Finally, every row until 21 sts remain.
Cast off 3 sts at the beginning of next 4 rows.
Cast off remaining stitches.

3 Work second side in the same manner.

4 Place the two knitted sections right sides together, and slip-stitch around the lower edge of the purse, from marker to marker.

5 Make the beaded fringe, using a beading or straw needle, by attaching a doubled length of strong cotton thread to the lower edge of the purse at one end of the seam-line. Thread on fifteen seed beads and one bugle, followed by a final seed bead. Take the beading needle back up through the bugle bead and seed beads to the lower edge of the purse, make several tiny over-sewing stitches to secure, pulling the thread until the top bead sits loosely against the fabric.

6 Take a small stitch to one side lower down the seamline and make another string of beads in the same manner. Continue to repeat this process until the lower edge of the purse is completely fringed.

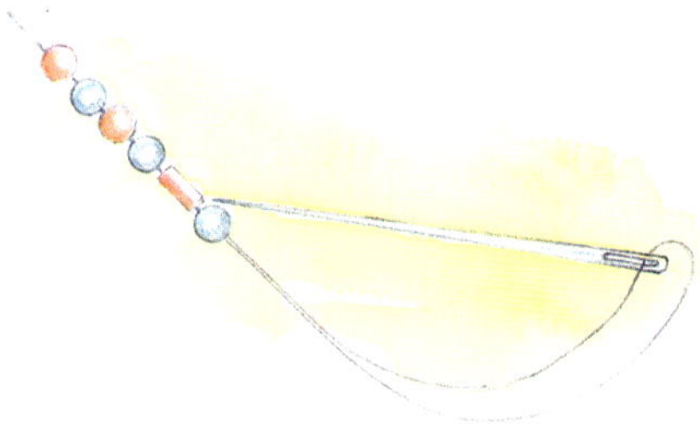

Making the fringe

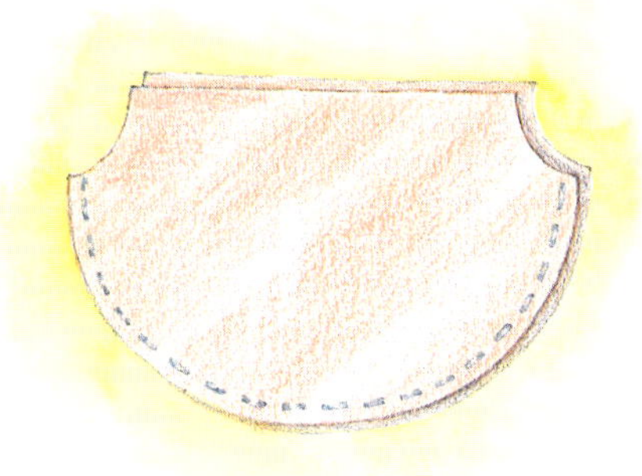

Stitching the lining

7 Finish off the thread by making a series of small straight stitches in one place, pull firmly and cut thread.

8 Using the knitted purse as a rough outline, draw a paper pattern shape. Cut this out and use to cut two lining pieces from silk or linen. Place fabric right sides together and machine stitch, as shown in the diagram.

9 Place the lining fabric inside the purse, wrong side of the lining to wrong side of purse, and slipstitch lining to purse along the top edge.

10 Place purse in position within the frame mount, gathering slightly if necessary, and, using a heavy-duty white thread, slipstitch firmly in place through the holes provided. On some frames the fabric needs to be pushed between the two lower edges which are then tapped down, using a hammer, to hold the fabric securely. Fasten off securely and cut thread.

BED THROW

The bed throw featured here has been adapted from a design of around 1900. The 110 squares needed (double-bed size) can be worked quickly using thick cotton yarn and a large crochet hook. By varying the number of squares, a throw of any size can be worked. The cotton yarn is available in a variety of colours, although white or cream would be most traditional and would blend with any decor. Matching cushions could also be made in the same or contrasting colours, using four or more squares. Each square requires about 2 balls of yarn.

MATERIALS

82 x 50g (1¾oz) Coats Lyric 8/8 in white, inc 10 balls for edging
6.0mm (UK size 4/US size 10) crochet hook
large-eyed darning needle

ABBREVIATIONS
For complete list of abbreviations and US conversions, see page 122.

Make 10 ch, ss into 1st chain to form a ring.

Row 1: 7 ch, miss 1 ch, 1 dbl tr [tr] into next ch, *3 ch, 1 dbl tr [tr] into ring, rep from * 5 times, ss to 4th ch of 7 ch lp, 4 ch;
Row 2: Into same ch, work 4 dbl tr [tr] 1 ch, *into next dbl tr [tr] work 5 dbl tr [tr], rep from * 6 times more, ss into top of previous 4 ch, 4 ch;
Row 3: Make a cluster by working 4 tr [dc] into next 4 tr [dc], leaving last two lps on hook each time, when last tr [dc] is worked draw last loop through all loops on hook to form a cluster, 8 ch *5 tr [dc] cl into next 5 tr [dc] group, 8 ch, rep from * 6 times more, ss to centre ch of last cl;
Row 4: Ss to 1st 8 ch lp, 3 ch, into lp work 9 tr [dc], *into next lp work 10 tr [dc], rep from * 7 times, 7 ch;
Row 5: 1 tr [dc] into same sp *miss 4 tr [dc], work 1 tr [dc] into next tr [dc], 3 ch, 1 tr [dc] into 5th tr [dc], 1 ch, work 1 tr [dc], 3 ch, 1 tr [dc] into next sp, rep from * to end, ss into 3rd ch of 1st tr [dc], 3 ch;

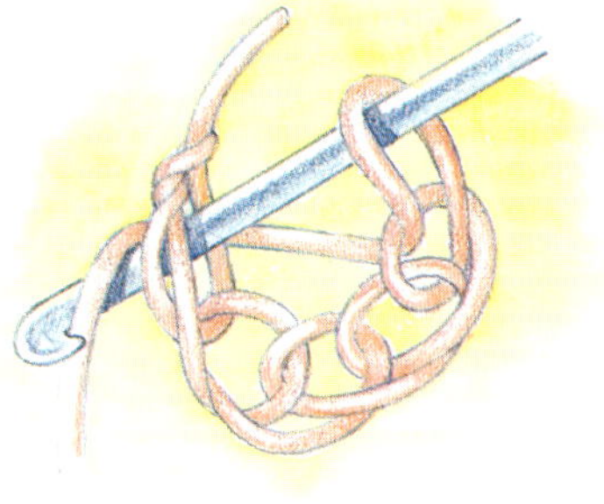

Slip stitch (a)

Row 6: Into 1st 3 ch lp work 2 tr [dc], 3 ch, 3 tr [dc], 3 ch, 3 tr [dc] into next 3 ch lp, rep 3 times, into next ch lp work 3 tr [dc], 3 ch, 3 tr [dc], rep from * 3 times, ss into 1st 3ch tr [dc], ss to corner lp, 3 ch;
Row 7: 2 tr [dc], 3 ch, 3 tr [dc] into corner lp, 3 ch *3 tr [dc] into next lp, 3 ch, rep 4 times, into corner work 3 tr [dc], 3 ch, 3 tr [dc], rep from * 3 times, ss to close and finish.

Chain stitch (a)

Slip stitch (b)

Work 110 squares (or sufficient for the size of bed throw required). Press the squares lightly using a steam iron. If necessary, the squares can be blocked out into shape whilst slightly damp. Place the squares on a large sheet or towel, several at a time, pin to shape, pulling the corners out if necessary, and leave until completely dry. Oversew the squares together using a large darning needle and Lyric yarn to make a rectangle 10 x 11 squares.

Chain stitch (b)

The new art of crochet was relatively quick to work and young ladies of the 19th century leisured classes must have seized upon this craft with pleasure. Traditionally, both in Great Britain and in the United States, a young woman should have at least one quilt in her bottom drawer, or hope chest, before she married. In some communities, thirteen was the requisite number, and the thirteenth would be a marriage quilt, containing a design of hearts - this would be placed on the couple's bed on the wedding night. With the advent of crochet, young women could now choose to work a coverlet in cotton thread, as a change from using traditional patchwork and quilting techniques.

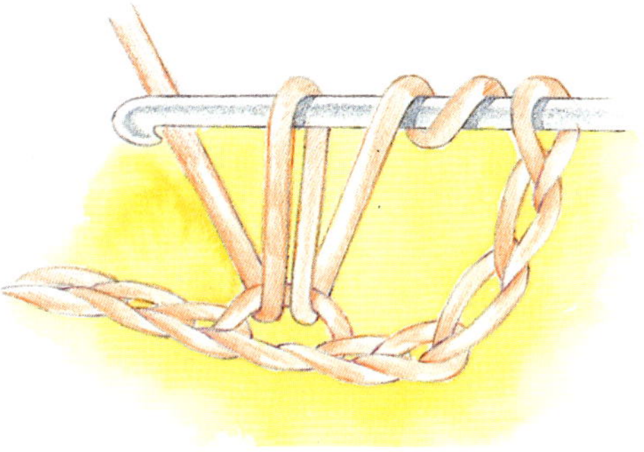

Treble crochet (double crochet) (a)

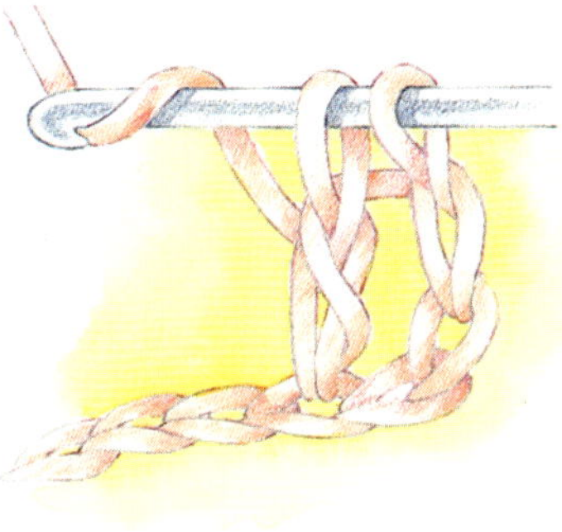

Treble crochet (double crochet) (b)

Treble crochet (double crochet) (c)

Border edging

Once the throw has been assembled, rejoin yarn at corner.

Row 1: Into corner work 6 dc [sc], then 1 dc [sc] into each ch along edge, work a further 6 dc [sc] into next corner, continue to end, ss to join, 3 ch;

Row 2: 1 tr [dc] into each dc [sc] to end, ss to join, 2 ch;

Row 3: (Picot edging) *1dc [sc], 3 ch, 1 dc [sc] into next ch, 2 dc [sc], 1 dc [sc] 3ch 1 dc [sc] into next ch to end, ss to join, fasten off.

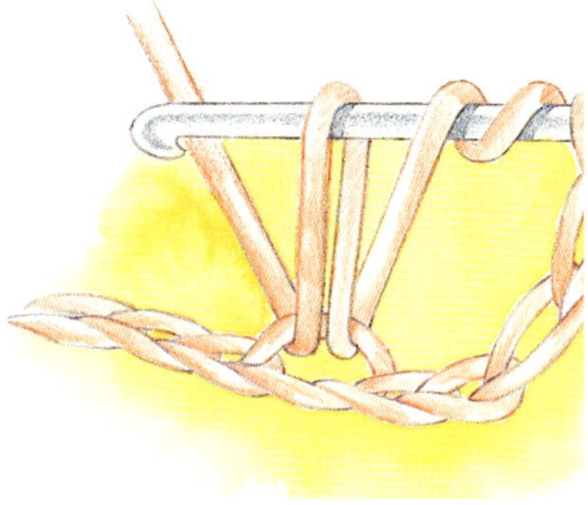

Double treble crochet (treble) (a)

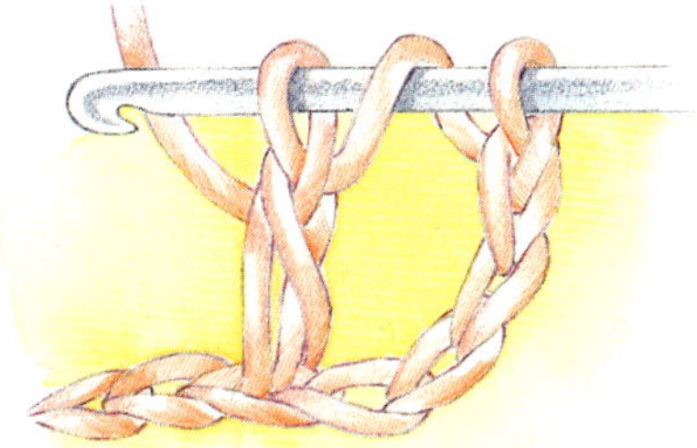

Double treble crochet (treble) (b)

Silver Celebrations

It seems most fitting to offer to a couple celebrating twenty-five years of marriage a gift made using needlework skills that have stood the test of time. Indeed, the design symbols on the Durham quilted cushion in this chapter were used for centuries in the small communities of northern England, Wales and Ireland, where patterns such as the Paisley pear and Weardale wheel have traditionally been combined with diagonal and straight lines to form seemingly complex arrangements. The silvery Ruskin work tablecloth has equally historic associations, but it makes use of a modern fabric to reduce the time and effort normally required for such intricate work.

DURHAM QUILTED CUSHION

The cushion shown here incorporates a simple design of lines and leaves around a central rosette and is relatively quick to work. Like all Durham quilting, it relies for its effect upon the play of light and shade created by the lines of running stitches. Here it has been worked on a medium-weight linen evenweave fabric, but, for extra drama, a smooth, shiny-surfaced cotton chintz or linen could be used (the sheen of the fabric would accentuate the stitching lines, bringing the pattern into higher relief). Early patterns would have been drawn out using a light scratch mark on the surface of the linen, but today's needleworkers can choose from a variety of specially developed markers, which wash away when the work is completed.

MATERIALS

two 40cm (16in) squares of evenweave linen
one 40cm (16in) square of medium-weight cotton wadding (batting)
one 40cm (16in) square of muslin
spool of white quilting thread
short 'sharps' needle
slate or tapestry frame
good-quality tracing paper
soft lead pencil
manilla card
embroidery marker pen
set square and ruler
all-purpose sewing thread
35cm (14in) cushion pad

1 Using a photocopier, enlarge the rosette and leaf patterns on page 120 by 140%. Then trace the outline using a soft lead pencil and tracing paper. Finally, transfer these outlines to manilla card and cut them out carefully to form templates.

2 Using the leaf template and the fabric marker pen, draw around the shape in each corner of one of the squares of linen, as shown in the illustration. Make sure to leave

Positioning leaf and rosette shapes, and stitching lines

12mm (1½ in) on all four sides for the seam allowance for assembling the cushion. Measure the linen carefully to find the centre point of the fabric and position the rosette template. Draw around this using the fabric marker pen and carefully draw in the petal outlines. Finally, using the set square and ruler, mark the diagonal and straight filling lines, as shown in the illustration.

3 Once the pattern has been completed, place the marked linen face down and place over it the square of wadding then the square of muslin. Pin together and stitch using long basting stitches, being sure to work through all the layers.

4 Attach fabric 'sandwich' securely to the slate or tapestry frame and stretch firmly before starting to work.

5 Take a 30cm (12in) length of single quilting thread and work the design using short straight running stitches through all thicknesses of fabric. Start and finish thread by running under a line of stitches already worked.

6 When the whole design has been completed, remove from frame. Measure and cut the second piece of linen into two pieces, measuring 15 x 40cm (6 x 16in) and 25 x 40cm (10 x 16in). Turn in and stitch a small hem along one long side of each piece. Overlap these two pieces to form an envelope face down over the quilting (see illustration).

7 Baste around the four edges of the cushion square, taking a 12mm (½in) seam allowance. Machine stitch, remove basting stitches and turn cushion cover right sides out. Wash cushion cover in hot water to slightly shrink the fabric and accentuate the stitching. Press lightly, if necessary, and insert cushion pad.

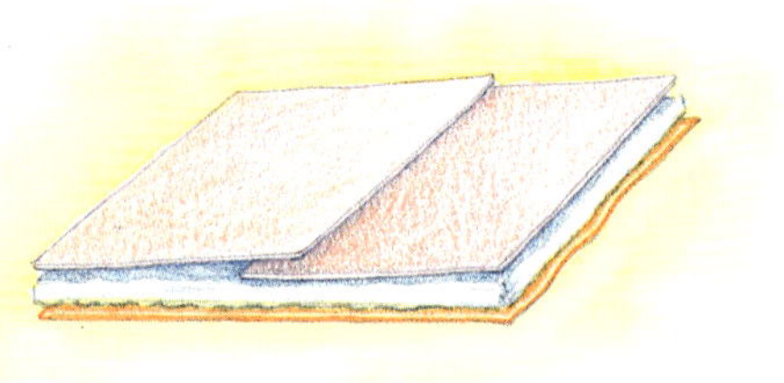

Assembling the cushion cover pieces.

Quilting was originally developed as a means of holding several layers of fabric together, providing warmth, decoration and protection. A continuous filling of carded wool was sandwiched between two layers of linen or silk and secured by a decorative line of stitching. Soldiers going into battle to face hand-to-hand combat would have been protected, even in early times, by tunics made in this fashion. The strength of the fabric thus produced would ward off glancing blows and give a surprising measure of protection. As the centuries passed, quilting became more specialised, and the quilt became a status symbol, displaying the wealth of its owner, through the quality of its fabric and stitching. At the other end of the social scale, quilting was also much practised by poor people as a means of recycling garments and precious fabric. Very often groups of women would gather together to produce one quilt at a time. Gossip, idle chatter and the occasional song or chanted rhyme would make the hours move more quickly and lighten the sometimes tedious work. Superstitions grew up surrounding the patterns and symbols which were universally recognised. A marriage quilt would, naturally, have one or more hearts worked into the design and would be used for the first time on the marriage bed. Such was the quality of the work and the firmness of the marriage bond, that these quilts were often used for the remainder of their owners' lives, to be passed on to the next generation as a symbol of marital harmony. It is, therefore, fitting to offer a gift of Durham quilting to any couple celebrating twenty-five years of marriage.

SILVER-AND-WHITE RUSKIN-WORK TABLECLOTH

The lovely silver-flecked fabric used for this anniversary tablecloth is complemented by the metallic silver threads used for the four-sided stitch border and the cross-stitch border. Though easy to work, it does require patience and good eyesight. Traditionally, fine linen is used for Ruskin work, but those new to this type of work will find the larger-scale fabric used here is easier. To complete the design, a simple line of cross-stitch and a corner motif of a single vine leaf have been worked just inside the hemline, giving a sophisticated and elegant highlight to an otherwise plain cloth. The beauty of the fabric will add its own undoubted impact to a gift that will be used again and again.

MATERIALS

2m (2½yd) of 140cm (55in)-wide Zweigart 20-count Bellana fabric, no. 1 silver fleck
dressmaker's shears
embroidery scissors
fine pins
all-purpose sewing thread in white
2 spools of Balger blending filament in silver
20 spools of Balger 1.5mm (1/16 in) fine ribbon in silver
No. 8 sharps and tapestry needles

MEASUREMENTS
Finished size: 180 x 120cm (71 x 47in)

1 Before beginning to work, the selvages of the fabric must be removed, as these might distort the cloth when washed. Cut off each selvage carefully and draw a thread along each cut edge to find a straight edge. Cut off any excess fabric.

2 Measure 5cm (2in) from one end of the fabric and, to make sure you have a straight edge, pull and withdraw a thread right across the fabric along the grain. Cut along the straight edge. At the opposite end of the fabric, pull and withdraw another thread to find the straight edge. Cut along this edge in the same way.

3 Measure in 30mm (1¼in) from each edge of the fabric and mark these points with a few pins. Taking a needle or pin, pick up the two threads of fabric which lie adjacent to the marker pins and parallel to each cut edge. These threads should be cut very carefully

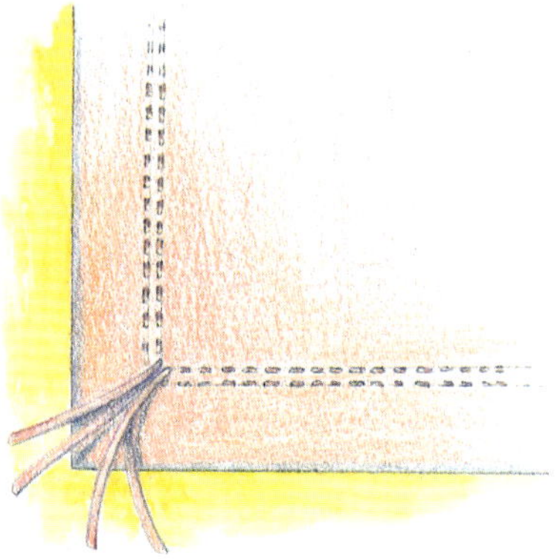

Withdrawing the first rows of threads

and withdrawn to within 30mm (1¼in) of each corner.

4 Turn the fabric over, right side down, on a flat surface. Fold over 6mm (¼in) on both long sides. Stitch this fold in place using long basting stitches and all-purpose thread.

5 Now fold the same edge over once again so that the first folded edge lies close to the drawn-thread line. Pin and tack (baste). Repeat along short sides of cloth, pinning and basting to within a short distance from each corner. Remove pins.

6 To neaten the corners, which in Ruskin work must be square, cut away 6mm (¼in) along the foldline on the long side only (see diagram).

7 Fold and baste (see diagram). Complete the other corners in the same manner.

8 Using all-purpose thread, slip-stitch hem, using tiny stitches. Remove basting stitches and press lightly, if necessary.

In comparison with Durham quilting, Ruskin work is a fairly new craft, although its origins can be found in drawn thread, cut linen and Renaissance needlepoint lace. Originally worked on handwoven linen, it can be practised on any evenweave commercially produced fabric. This craft owes its development to the work of John Ruskin, who took an interest in the linen industry when he moved north to the Lake District in 1872. There he set about encouraging a cottage industry that would improve the lives of his poorer neighbours; he and his housekeeper, Marion Twelves, devoted themselves to providing teaching, equipment, new designs and patterns. Ruskin work has, to some extent, fallen from popularity, but it is a delightful and rewarding craft which deserves its place amongst the heirlooms we are creating today.

Neatening the corners

9 From the withdrawn threads of the hemline, count four threads then remove the next two threads, leaving the corners undrawn.

10 Carefully withdraw all cut threads to the corners and, using a tapestry needle, weave these threads into the hemline, so that they are unnoticeable.

11 Using a tapestry needle and blending filament, work four-sided stitch along the two rows of drawn threads all around the cloth. Work over four threads at a time, with a slight tension that will pull the threads together sufficiently to leave a small hole at each side, but not so much that the hem begins to crinkle (see diagram). Should the number of threads at the corners be uneven, simply work over the remaining three or five threads in the normal manner, turn the cloth and continue along the next side. When finishing a length

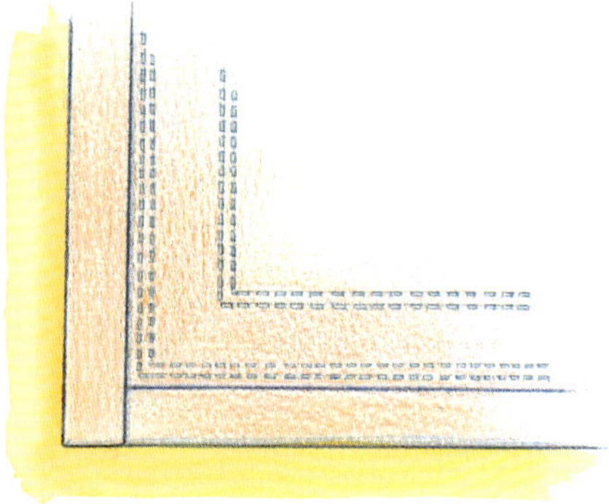

Withdrawing the next rows of threads

of thread, work a few oversewing stitches in the centre of the closest block and cut the thread. Start a new thread in the same manner.

12 Count seven threads in from the four-sided stitch, and work a single line of cross stitch around the cloth, in fine ribbon, across two threads of the fabric.

13 Counting twelve threads in from each edge of one corner, cross-stitch the vine-leaf motif using the fine ribbon. Start at the point indicated on the chart by arrow and work each stitch over two threads of fabric. Repeat the same design in the other three corners.

14 Once completed, the cloth can be washed or dry cleaned following the manufacturer's instructions.

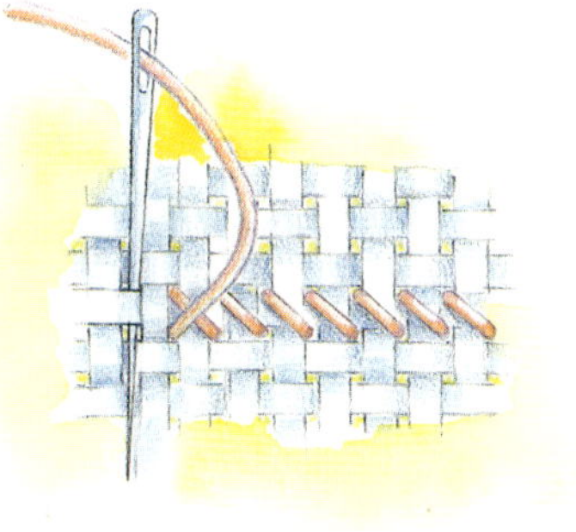

Cross stitch (a)

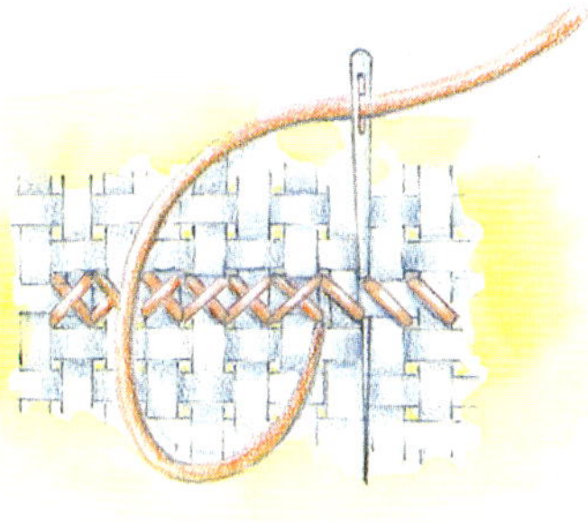

Cross stitch (b)

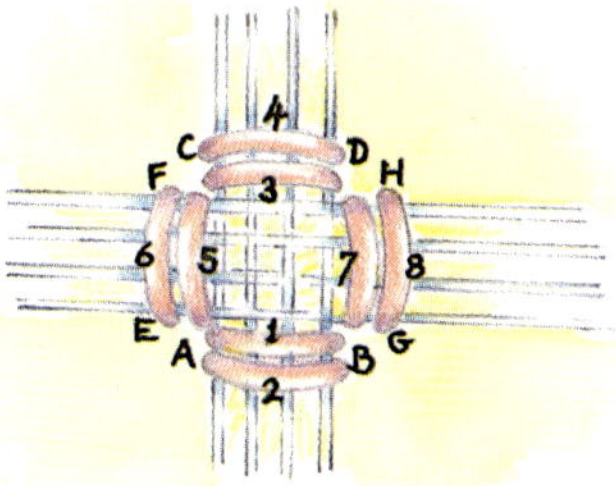

Four-sided stitch

KEY

☒ **Balger fine ribbon in silver**

THE GOLDEN YEARS

Everyone must agree that fifty years of marriage should be marked by a gift in keeping with the importance of a golden wedding anniversary. This chapter's spray of golden silk roses, beaded and embroidered ring box and floral needlepoint footstool are all particularly appropriate gifts, to be worked with love and respect for the happy couple's lifetime achievement. After such a long time together, the couple are likely to have all the basic essentials, and even luxuries, of home life, so it is a pleasure to give gifts which are decorative rather than functional – and can be displayed with pride.

EMBROIDERED RING BOX WITH GOLD THREADS AND BEADS

This tiny ring box is just large enough to take two golden rings, symbols of the love and devotion of a couple who have weathered fifty years together. It is not too difficult to work and could be personalised with initials and dates. Our box has been made in a gold damask fabric and decorated with stem stitch and gold beads, but any combination of beading and stitching could be worked, depending on your own preferences. Grey board is obtainable from good art supply shops and some printers and picture framers. It is strong and durable and is ideal for making boxes. Once the technique has been mastered, you can adapt the measurements to make square or rectangular boxes of any suitable size. The box could also be worked in any number of colour combinations such as silvers and purples, or dark greens to commemorate other anniversaries or occasions.

MATERIALS

metal ruler
HB pencil
sheet of grey board
set square
cutting board
heavy-duty craft knife
scalpel
30cm (12in) gold felt
30 x 30cm (12 x 12in) of silk upholstery fabric in gold
30 x 30cm (12 x 12in) of matching upholstery fabric
spool of pure silk gold embroidery thread/floss
approximately 100 gold glass seed beads
4 gold glass bugle beads
1 medium-sized cream bead
1 gold star-shaped sequin
1 metre (1yd) of gold braid trim
reel of gold all-purpose sewing thread
fabric adhesive
dressmaker's scissors
fine needlework scissors
fine curved upholstery needle
0.25 metre (¼yd) of light weight wadding (batting)
sheet of lightweight white card
fine paintbrush

1 Using the ruler and lead pencil draw out two rectangles measuring 5.5 x 4cm (2⅛ x 1½in) and two rectangles measuring 5 x 4cm (2 x ½in) on to the grey board. Use the set square to check that the angles are correct before cutting.

2 Cut out each rectangle carefully using the heavy-duty craft knife fitted with a new blade. Do not use too much pressure: several shallow cuts will be more effective and accurate. As you finish cutting, check that each pair of rectangles matches perfectly.

3 The short edges of each rectangle must now be mitred on the inside. Draw a line approximately 4mm (⅛ in) from each edge. Holding the metal ruler along this line, shave off a small amount of board using the scalpel, to produce a sloping edge.

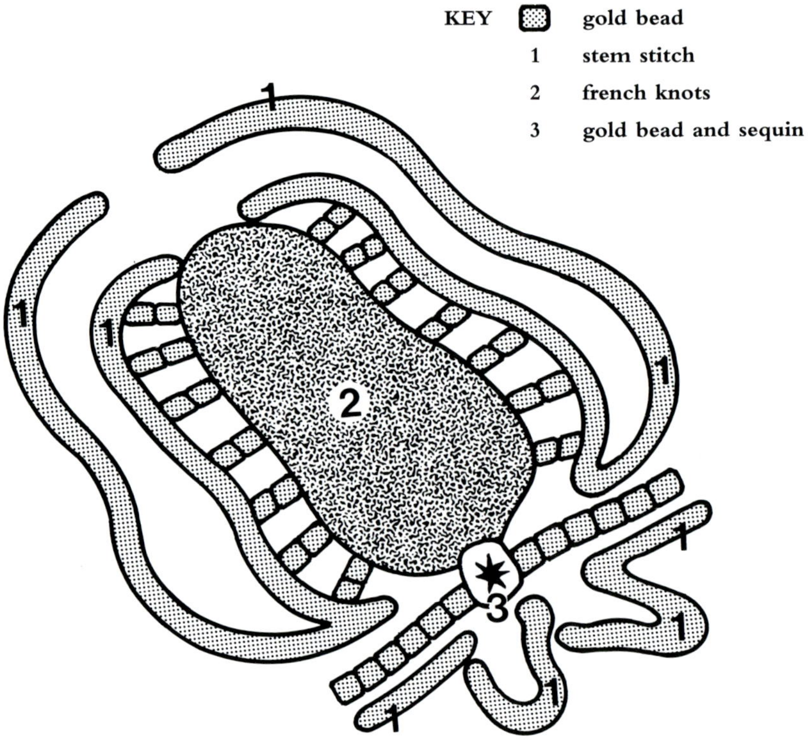

4 Lay the gold felt flat on a smooth surface and place the rectangles in a line across it, with the mitred edges touching and facing upwards. Carefully lift each rectangle and paint the outside thinly and evenly with adhesive. Replace and press down. Leave to dry thoroughly.

5 Using dressmaker's scissors, cut roughly around the felt, and then trim close to the grey board using fine embroidery scissors.

6 Press the silk fabric carefully to remove all creases. Lay it flat, right side down. Place the rectangles over this, felt side down. Carefully trim the fabric, leaving a turning allowance of 1cm (1/2in) all around.

7 Place a small amount of adhesive along each side of the grey board, approximately 4mm (1/8in) from each edge. Turn the seam allowance over the top and bottom long edges, pulling the fabric slightly to prevent puckering. Press the fabric down until firmly stuck to the board.

8 Fold and mitre each corner and turn over seam allowance on both short edges. Dry thoroughly.

9 Using the sewing thread and curved needle, ladderstitch the two short edges together to form the sides of the box. Stitch this edge twice and finish off with a few tiny oversewing stitches.

Layering the fabric, felt and card

10 Decide which is the top of the box and measure the rectangle produced by the four sides. This will vary from box to box and must be measured precisely.

11 Draw out this rectangle on to grey board, and cover with a thin layer of adhesive and wadding (batting). Trim as before.

12 Using a photocopier, reduce the design (left) by 50% and then transfer the design to the silk fabric. Alternatively, find your own favourite motif which will sit centrally on the top of the box. Embroider the outline of the motif in gold thread and stem stitch, and decorate with the sequins and seed beads.

13 Making sure that the embroidered motif is central, cover the lid with the embroidered silk fabric, mitring the corners and keeping the adhesive away from the front of the fabric. Check that the wadding (batting) is smooth.

14 Push the lid of the box into place and ladderstitch in position, using the sewing thread and curved needle. Work around the top of the box twice for added strength. This then becomes the large lid of the ring box.

15 Now, cut two rectangles measuring 5.5 x 2cm (2 1/8 x

Stem stitch

¾in) and two rectangles 5 x 2cm (2 x ¾in). These will form the base of the ring box. Assemble as before, covering the base with felt, not wadding (batting).

16 To make the fabric hinge, cut a rectangle of silk fabric measuring approximately 7 x 4.5cm (2¾ x 1¾in) and fold this wrong side out to form a tube. Machine stitch the shorter cut edges together, press open the seam and turn right side out. This tube should then be pressed flat, with the seam running in the centre.

17 Glue this fabric hinge in position, in the inner back wall of the base and lid boxes, making sure that the stitched corners of the base and lid are to the back, and that the hinge lies centrally.

18 From the lightweight card, cut five rectangles to line the box lid. First, measure the internal dimensions of the box lid and cut a card lining for this. Cover with gold upholstery fabric as before, omitting the felt, and glue into position as the inner lid lining.

19 To make a cushion on which the rings can sit, cut sufficient wadding (batting) to fill the base of the box. Cover with gold silk and glue this into position to form a padded base.

20 Make a golden tassel by stringing one seed bead, followed by one bugle bead then eight seed beads on to gold thread, five times. Draw the threads through a medium-sized bead, and stitch them to the centre of the lower edge of the box lid. Glue bands of gold braid around the box base and lid and leave to dry thoroughly before use.

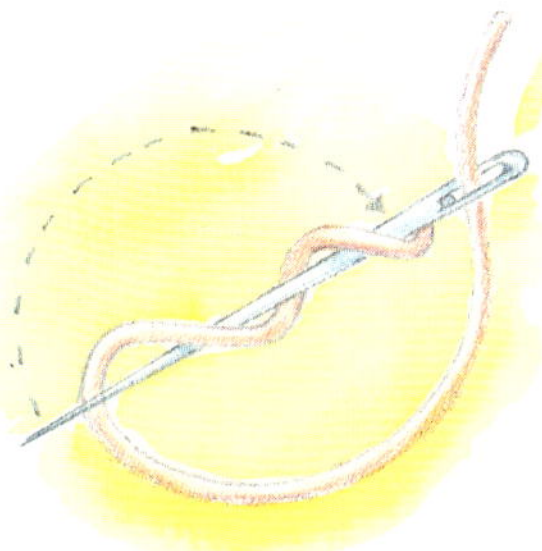

French knot (a)

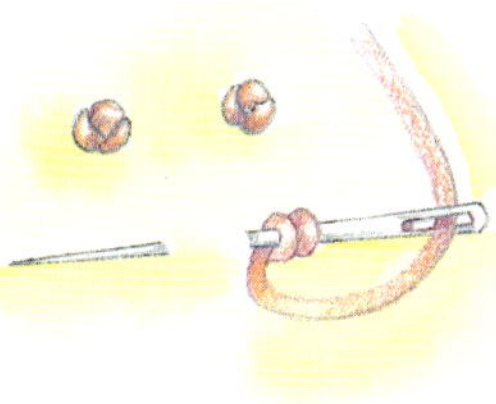

French knot (b)

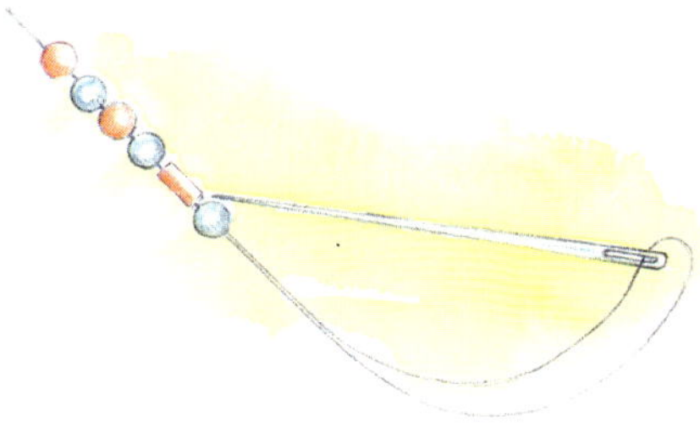

Making the bead tassel

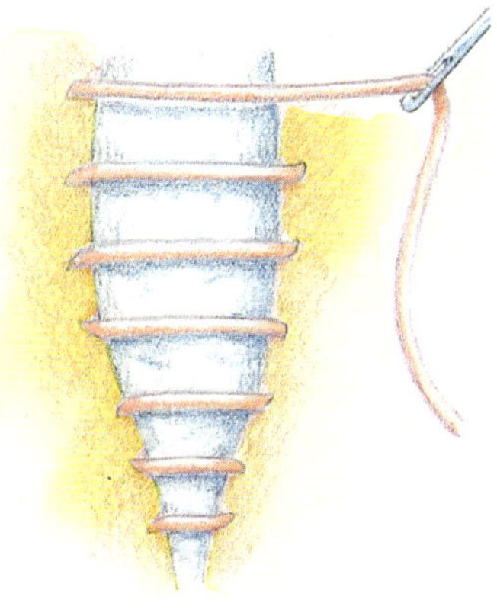

Ladderstitch

SPRING POSY FOOTSTOOL

This needlepoint footstool is decorated with a posy of spring flowers, specially designed by Christina Marsh, to make the perfect golden wedding gift. Pansies and anemones are mixed with forsythia to give a golden glow, and interwoven with forget-me-nots symbolising true love, violets for faithfulness and ivy for fidelity. Worked in tent stitch on canvas using one strand of tapestry wool, this project uses straight-forward basic needlepoint techniques, though, if you are new to needlepoint, it is a good idea to practise first on a scrap of canvas.

MATERIALS

40cm x 40cm (16in x16in) of 12-count mono interlock canvas
tapestry needle size 20
fabric marker
rectangular tapestry frame
wooden footstool, 28cm (11in) diameter
Anchor tapestry wool (yarn) as shown in the chart key - one skein of each, with the following exceptions:
6 x 9112 (apple green background),
3 x 9104 (dark green),
2 x 9102 (medium green),
2 x 8120 (gold)

1 Find the centre of the canvas by folding it in half, then half again and making a single stitch where the folds cross. Draw a circle in the centre of the canvas, with a diameter of 30.5cm (12in).

2 Mount the canvas in a tapestry frame making sure it is evenly tensioned. Starting at the centre point, work the design in tent stitch, using one strand and following the chart on page 86. Complete each flower before starting another, and avoid taking surplus thread from one area to another across the back.

3 When the design is complete, start the background, preferably working in diagonal rows as this will minimise distortion and make the stitching more even. Work to the edge of the circle.

4 Remove from the stitching frame. Stretch the canvas if necessary and mount into the footstool according to the manufacturer's instructions.

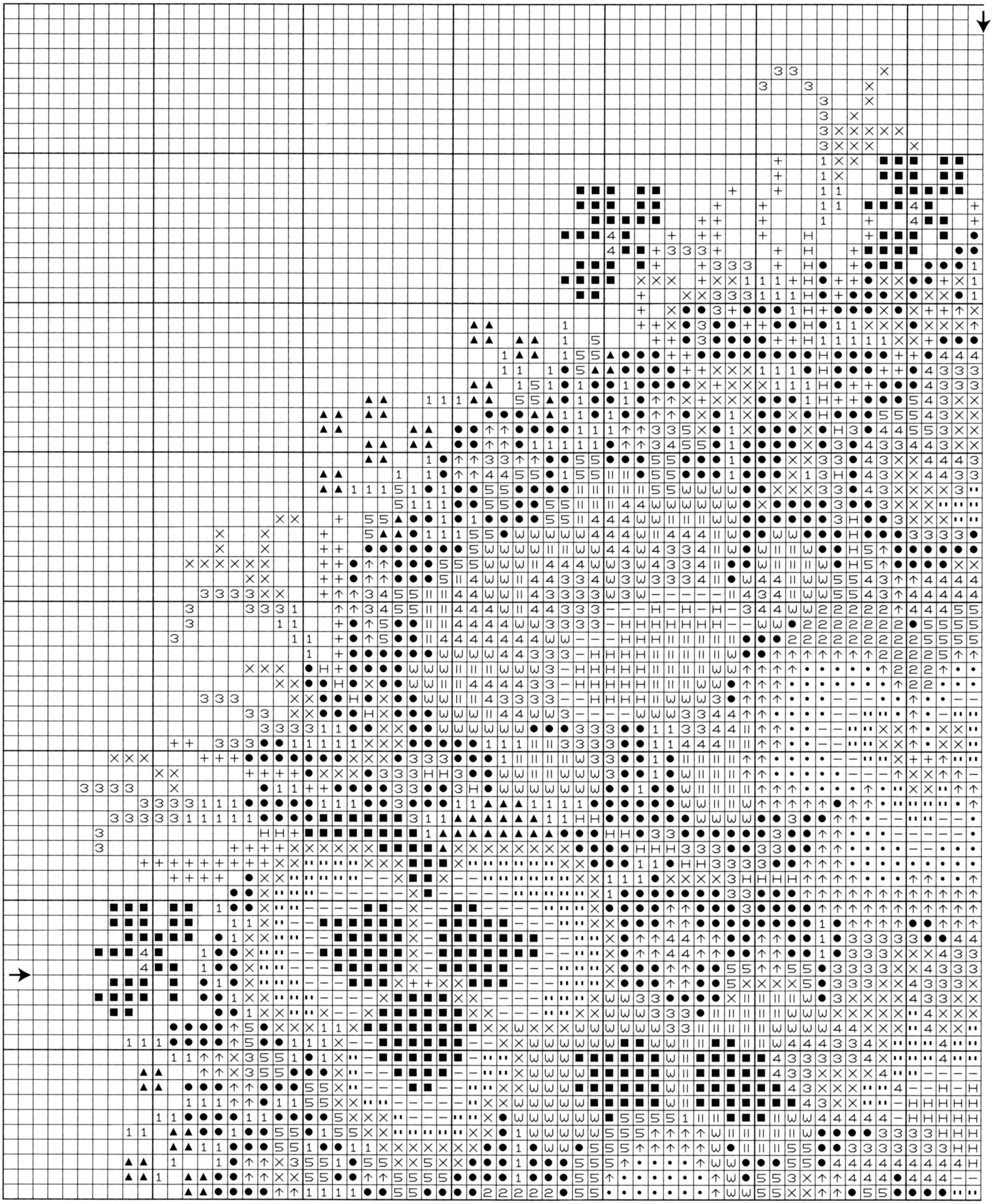

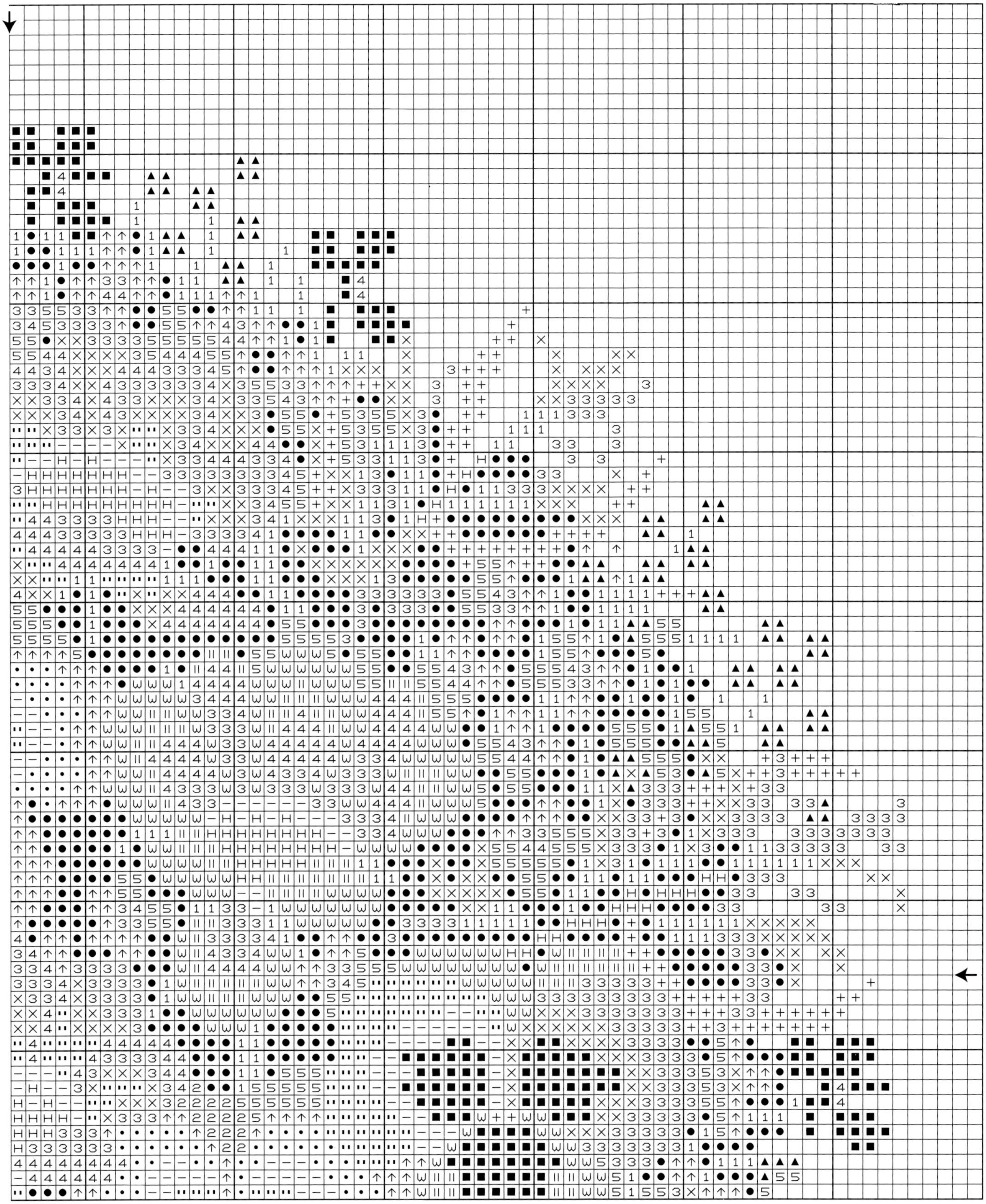

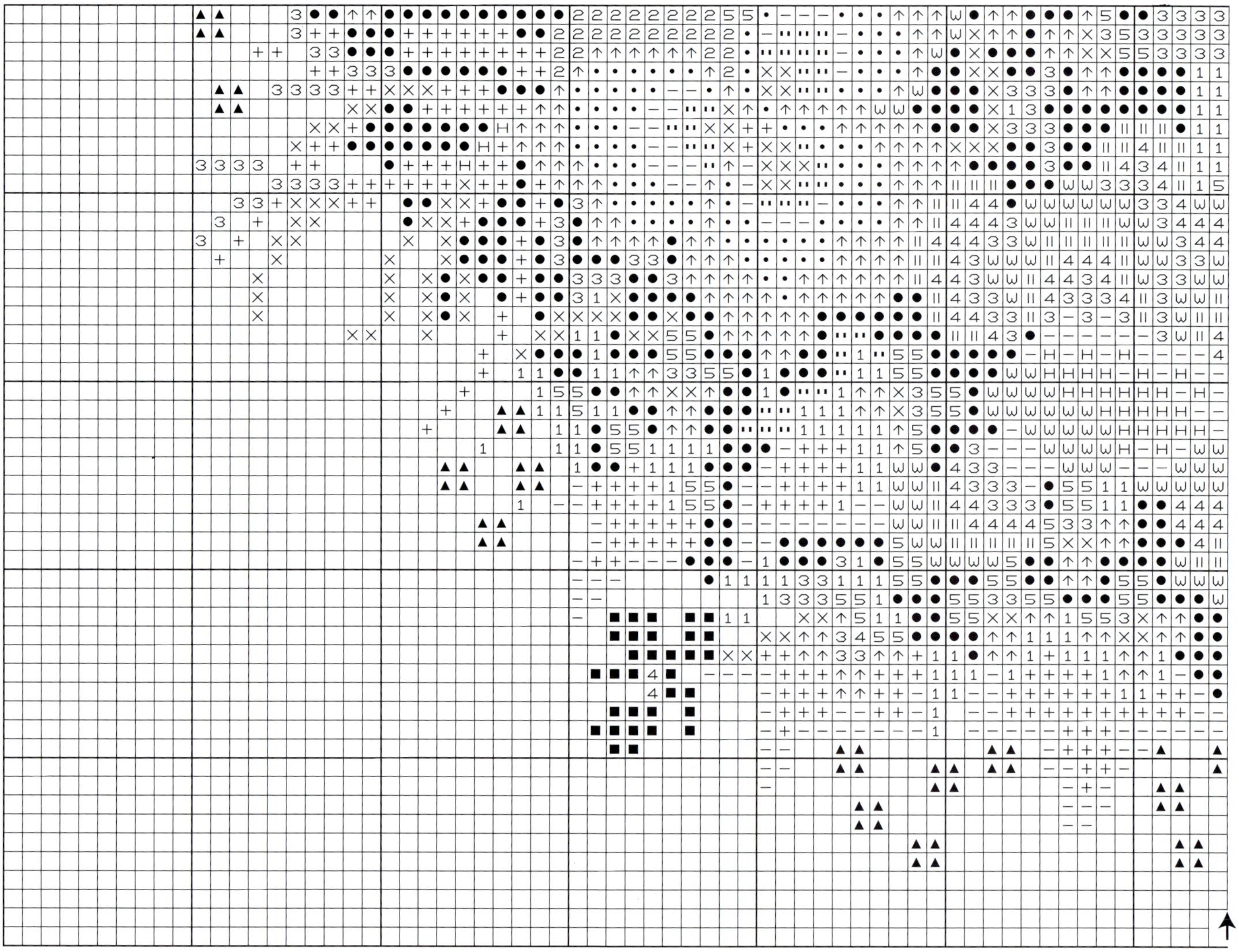

Tent stitch (a)

Tent stitch (b)

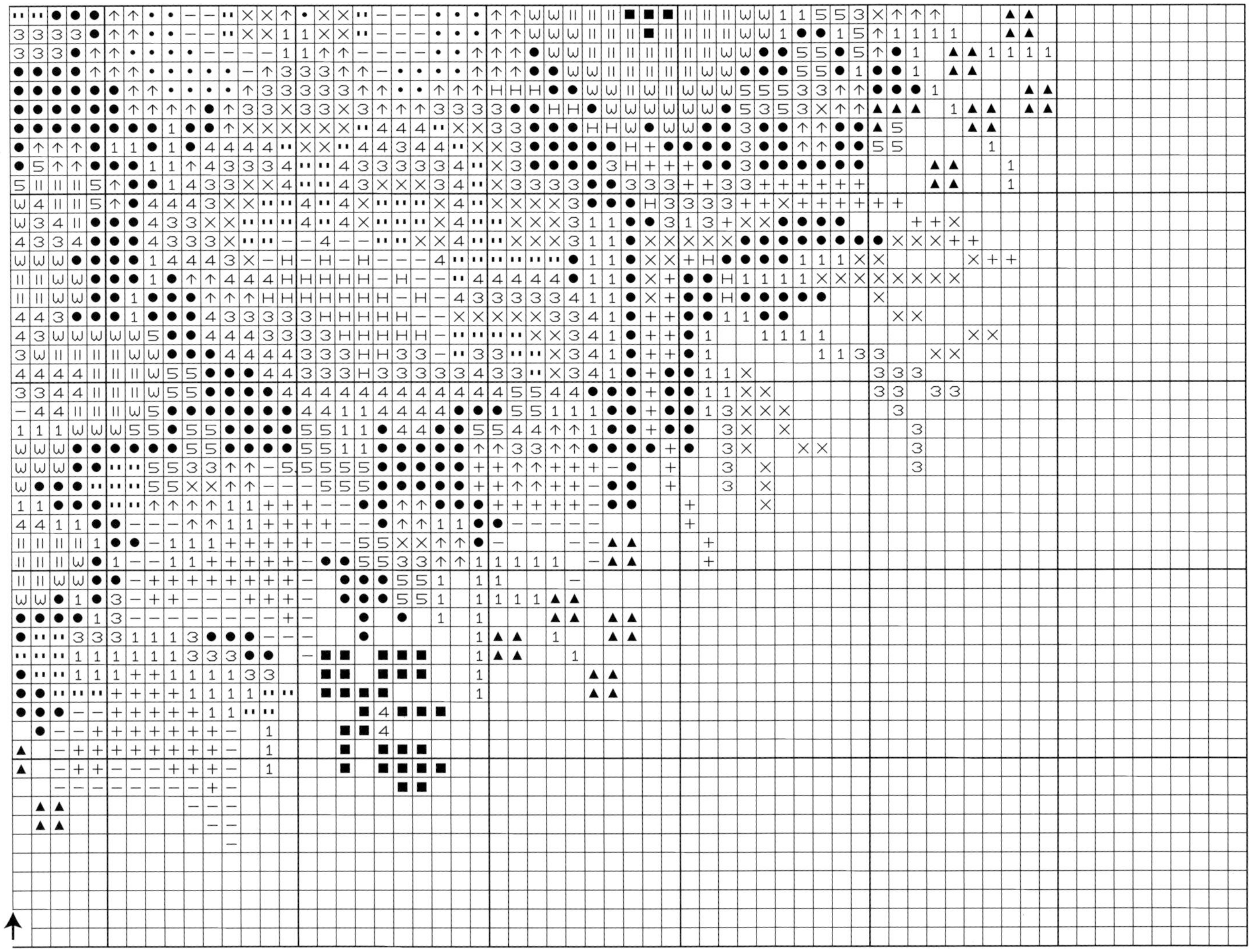

KEY

Anchor tapestry wool

Symbol	Colour	Number
W	White	8000
4	Medium green	9102
×	Dark brown	9644
–	Lilac	8588
5	Medium orange	8154
•	Gold	8120
1	Light yellow	8116
H	Light blue	8776
2	Dark blue	8632
‖	Light green	9100
3	Dark green	9104
▪▪	Purple	8594
↑	Dark orange	8156
▲	Orange	8124
+	Yellow	8118
●	Lemon	8112
■	Medium blue	8628

Background: Apple green 9112

EMBROIDERED PANEL OF GOLDEN ROSES

Combining traditional elements associated with a golden wedding, our panel of silken roses will bring lasting pleasure. In the language of flowers, while a single rose signifies 'love', a garland of roses offers the reward of merit, a fitting token for this occasion. The message is combined with gold, in this case only gold thread, though the real thing is an age-old gift representing purity and abundance. The simple surface stitchery used to create this panel has been enhanced by the precious sheen of pure silk thread, and given depth by subtle shading. The fineness and delicacy of this work will express to its recipients all the esteem and love of its maker and giver.

MATERIALS

35 x 35cm (14 x 14in) of silk gauze in ecru
40 x 40cm (16 x 16in) cork board, minimum measurement
drawing pins or thumb tacks
tracing paper
masking tape
soft lead pencil
hard lead pencil
heavy-duty linen thread
30 x 13cm (12 x 5in) rectangular embroidery frame
size 10 embroidery needle
embroidery scissors
mounting card
25 x 25cm (10 x 10in) of apricot-pink moiré silk upholstery fabric
gold mount card, cut to drop into back of frame
19 x 16.5cm (7½ x 6½in) gold frame
Mulberry Silk embroidery threads set 'On Golden Pond' *or* 1 spool each thread as listed in the key

MEASUREMENTS

Completed embroidery measures 108 x 108mm (4¼ x 4¼in)

1 Turn in and baste a fairly wide hem, approx 12mm (½in) all around the square of gauze.

2 Using a photocopier, reduce the design diagram on page 93 to 60%. If you are confident of your embroidery skills, trace just the basic outlines onto tracing paper. If in any doubt, trace all the areas for the different stitches. These will provide your guide and give details of colour and thickness of threads and also the type of stitch used in the original design.

3 Using drawing pins or thumb tacks, stretch the silk gauze onto the cork board, making sure to secure at each corner, through the folded hem. Centre the tracing paper face down over the gauze and secure using masking tape around all sides.

4 Transfer the design to the gauze by redrawing over the outlines, using a hard lead pencil. When all

MANUFACTURING
WELLERS & SILVERSMITHS
USSELL (Sheffield) Ltd
4. NEW STREET
BIRMINGHAM

KEY

Mulberry silk emboidery threads

1	light gold	E104	chain stitch, double row
2	light gold	E104	satin stitch
3	old gold	E102	satin stitch
4	pale pink	S165	long and short stitch
5	cream	S27	long and short stitch
6	primrose	F326	satin stitch
7	caramel	S412	french knots
8	pale yellow	W327	satin stitch
9	pale yellow	W327	chain stitch, double row
10	lemon	S325	long and short stitch
11	dark rose	K846	chain stitch, double row
12	medium rose	W587	satin stitch
13	light rose	W586	satin stitch
14	dove grey	S653	satin stitch
15	grey green	K506	french knots
16	caramel	S412	french knots
17	tangerine	S300	satin stitch
18	medium green	F397	chain stitch
19	light green	S355	chain stitch
20	leaf green	S432	stem stitch
21	dark green	S398	chain stitch
22	dark green	S398	stem stitch
23	medium olive green	W596	chain stitch
24	cream	S27	satin stitch
25	dark green	S398	satin stitch
26	apricot gold	F932	chain stitch
27	apricot gold	F932	satin stitch
28	light rose	W586	french knots

For centuries the very finest embroideries, designed for royalty and religious purposes, have been worked in silk threads. The Imperial Court of China, which for generations protected the secret of the silkworm, must surely offer the most delicate and delightful of all silken textiles. Silk gauze is a very beautiful and fragile fabric, which can easily become damaged whilst being worked. It is, however, worth the extra care involved as its translucent shimmer will lift your work into another dimension. Also, the silk threads used here are of different thicknesses, which helps to give a three dimensional effect. For those who find working with silk too expensive or tiresome, this bouquet of flowers can be worked on any fine-count (32 or more) evenweave fabric, such as linen, using cotton thread. A thread conversion chart can be found on page 123. When using cotton threads, vary the number of strands used, to mimic the effect created by different thicknesses of silk.

REDUCE TO 60%

Chain stitch

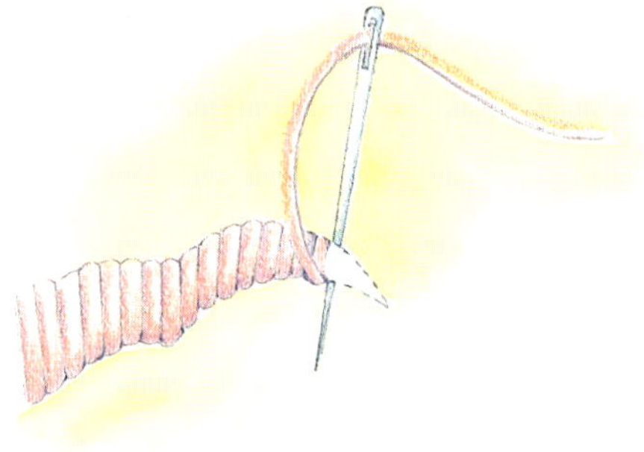

Satin stitch

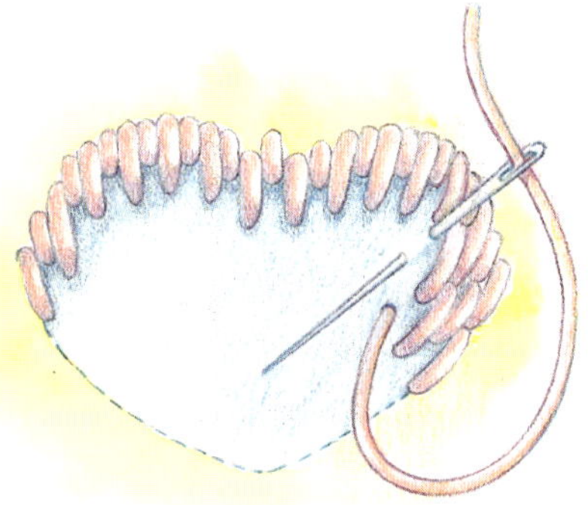

Long-and-short stitch

the design lines have been drawn, remove the masking tape and tracing paper. Check that the design is complete before removing the drawing pins or thumb tacks.

5 The fabric can now be attached to the embroidery frame. Silk gauze will stretch slightly as it is worked, so it is essential to make it as taut as possible at this stage. Although this fabric looks very fragile, it will withstand a certain amount of pressure, but beware of tearing. Once the fabric is stretched evenly in all directions, finish off with a few oversewing stitches and clip the thread. You are now ready to begin working the design.

6 If using the recommended silk threads, follow the design diagram given on page 93, working in chain, stem, satin, and long-and-short stitch. The centre of each rose is composed of French knots. For those who prefer to work with cotton threads, a conversion chart can be found on page 123. When using silk gauze, it is essential that your work be as neat as possible; all thread tails must be sewn into the back of a block of stitches to prevent them showing on the front of the work.

7 Begin each flower from its centre (the oval of French knots) and work outwards, until the first row of satin stitch has been worked in each petal. Then work two rows of chain stitch around each petal outline, before finishing with the other rows of long-and-short stitch and satin-stitch shading. The accuracy of this stitching is crucial to the finished look of your embroidery and it will help to count threads at this stage, working a satin stitch between each two threads. The leaves and stems have been worked in a selection of stem and chain stitch.

8 Once the whole design has been worked, remove the holding stitches carefully from the sides of the frame. Loosen the wing nuts and unwind the rollers. Remove basting stitches from the holding tapes at the top and bottom of your frame, leaving the basting stitches which hold the hem.

9 Should your silk embroidery require washing, do this by swishing it gently in tepid water, to which a few drops of liquid detergent have been added. Rinse well with plenty of cool water and lay the embroidery out to dry on a fluffy towel. The gauze can then be ironed with a cool iron, over the back of the work, on a clean towel, to prevent the stitching from being flattened.

10 Stretch completed embroidery over the rectangle of gold mounting card, which has been cut to the correct size to fit the frame. Hold in place with a series of long stitches across the back of the mounting card, using heavy-duty thread and darning needle. When the embroidery is properly stretched it can be placed in the frame and the frame assembled.

J
25.12.95
8m

A FAMILY CHRISTMAS

Everyone loves a family Christmas, and in most families there is a special emphasis on traditions that are unique and very personal. Why not add to the enjoyment, by producing one or all of our delightful heirlooms, specifically designed to bring pleasure both in the making and the giving. The festivities we associate with a modern-day Christmas celebration have been drawn from many cultures and civilizations. Unrecognised by many, the symbols held dear by the Christian faith have been borrowed from earlier, often pagan, beliefs. The Christmas tree, brought to England from Germany by Prince Albert to represent the light of Christ in a world of darkness, can be traced in origin both to the Tree of Life of Norse mythology and to the Tree of Light in Jewish religious teaching. However, it was in 19th century Britain that the varied strands of myth and belief were woven together to make the most popular family occasion of the year.

CHRISTMAS TREE DECORATIONS

No Christmas is complete without a beautifully decorated tree, and nothing can beat the charm of handmade decorations such as these. You can make these baubles, designed by Elizabeth Hunt, in the traditionally festive red, green and gold as shown here, or adapt them to match your existing decorations. Extra decorations will make equally stunning additions to festive displays of foliage and table decorations throughout the house.

MATERIALS
Gold, Red and Green Ball

7cm (2¾in) diameter foam ball
transparent sewing thread
gold spray paint
tracing paper
soft pencil
gold thread
12cm (5in) gold cord
50cm (20in) gold braid, 12mm (½in) wide
20cm (8in) red satin ribbon, 8cm (3in) wide
20cm (8in) green satin ribbon, 8cm (3in) wide
45cm (½yd) narrow loop-edged red ribbon
45cm (½yd) narrow loop-edged green ribbon
2 red 12mm (½in) flower sequins
2 green 12mm (½in) flower sequins
4 red 10mm (⅜in) sequins
4 green 10mm (⅜in) sequins
4 red 12mm (¼in) sequins
4 green 12mm (¼in) sequins
20 small pearl beads

1 Spray the foam ball with gold paint and leave to dry.

2 Make a loop of gold cord and stitch to the seam of the ball.

3 Divide the surface of the ball into four sections by sewing two lengths of gold braid around the circumference, fastening them neatly at the loop.

4 Trace the template (page 121) for the decorative panels. Cut two red and two green shapes on the bias, from the wide ribbon.

5 Stitch a red flower sequin and pearl bead onto the centre of both red panels. Stitch green flower sequins and pearl beads onto the green panels. Stitch two red sequins onto the green panels and two green sequins onto the red panels above and below the flower sequins.

6 Stitch the red panels to opposite sides of the ball using invisible thread. Stitch the green panels to the other sides.

7 Stitch red looped ribbon down the edges of the green panels and green ribbon down the edges of the red panels, attaching a sequin at top and bottom to cover the joins.

MATERIALS
Red Suede Heart

- **tracing paper**
- **soft pencil**
- **15 x 30cm (6 x 12in) red suede or red cotton velvet**
- **matching red sewing thread**
- **10 x 30cm (4 x 12in) cotton fabric**
- **26 silver 6mm (¼in) sequins**
- **26 silver-lined 3mm (⅛in) glass bugle beads**
- **10 x 30cm (4 x 12in) medium quilting interlining for backing, plus extra for stuffing**
- **50cm (20in) narrow gold cord, 3mm (⅛in) wide**

1 Trace the heart template (page 121) on to paper. Mark the quilting lines.

2 Cut two hearts from red suede or velvet. Tailor tack the quilting and stitching lines.

3 Place a layer of interlining and cotton backing onto the wrong side of each piece of red fabric.

4 Carefully machine stitch along the quilting lines shown on the template. Trim the interlining and the backing fabric to fit the suede.

5 Stitch a sequin and pearl bead into the centre of each square.

6 Baste the two halves of the heart right sides together and machine stitch, leaving an opening to turn the heart inside out.

7 Stuff with a little extra interlining and slipstitch the gap closed.

8 Stitch gold cord around the edge, finishing with a loop at the top.

MATERIALS
Gold Net Ball

- 7cm (2¾in) diameter foam ball
- gold spray paint
- 12cm (5in) gold cord
- circle of gold net, 14cm (5½in) in diameter
- gold thread
- 1m (1yd) red ribbon, 6mm (¼in) wide
- silver 12mm (½in) flower sequin
- small pearl bead
- 60 silver-lined 3mm (⅛in)bugle beads

1 Spray the foam ball with gold paint and leave to dry.

2 Make a loop out of gold cord and stitch it to the seam of the ball.

3 Using the gold thread, make a line of running stitches around the circle of gold net, about 25mm (1in) from the edge, then gather and draw up around ball, finishing with secure stitches around the cord loop.

4 Cut three equal 22cm (8½in) lengths of red ribbon. Stitch them together in the centre, adding a flower sequin and pearl in the centre (see diagram).

5 Stitch glass beads to the ribbons at 1cm (⅜in) intervals.

6 Stitch the centre of the ribbons, with flower sequin, to the base of the foam ball. Stitch the ends of the ribbons neatly to the top of the ball. Finish with a red ribbon bow, concealing the ribbon ends.

Decorating the ribbon

MATERIALS
Gold Star

tracing paper
soft pencil
basting thread
20cm (1/4yd) gold lame
gold thread
45cm (1/2yd) narrow gold cord
2 gold 15mm (5/8in) flower sequins
2 small pearl beads
4 silver 2cm (3/4in) double sequins
1m (1yd) iridescent 0.5cm (1/4in) sequin strip
small quantity stuffing

1 Trace the star template on page 121, marking the stitching lines.

2 Using this pattern, cut two stars from gold lame. Mark the stitching lines with basting stitches.

3 Place the two star pieces right sides facing, and machine stitch around the outside, leaving a small gap for turning. Trim the seams as marked.

4 Turn the star right sides out. Carefully push out the points, and stuff - quite lightly to make it possible to stitch through the whole star when stuffed.

5 Slipstitch the opening, and baste through the centre of the star to hold it firm.

6 Machine stitch out from the centre five times, following the stitching lines.

7 Make a loop from gold cord and stitch it to one of the points of the star. Sew five sequin strips from the centre out to the points, on both sides. In the centre of the star on both sides, place a flower sequin on top of a double silver sequin, and stitch on with a pearl bead in the centre. Pull the stitching firmly to draw in the centre.

MATERIALS
Three-sided Bauble with Tassel

- tracing paper and soft pencil
- 10cm (4in) cream silk fabric
- 45cm (½yd) gold braid
- scrap of gold lamé
- 1m (1yd) narrow gold cord
- 45cm (½yd) thick gold cord
- 3 red 12mm (½in) flower sequins
- 6 green 12mm (½in) flower sequins
- 6 gold 1cm (⅜in) petalled sequins
- 15 small pearl beads
- stuffing
- invisible thread
- fabric glue

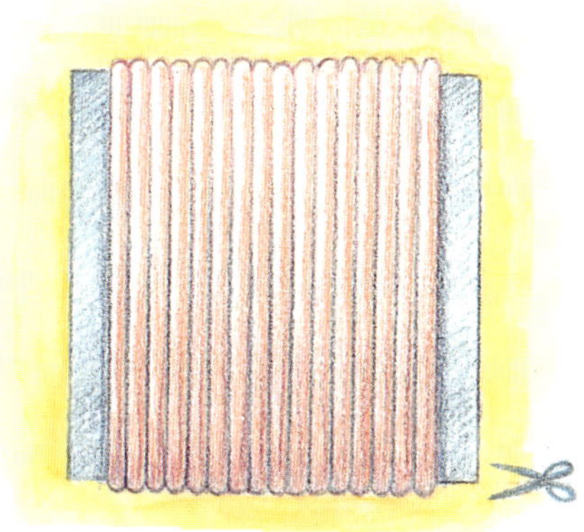

Making a tassel (a)

1 Trace the main template (page 121), and cut three pieces on the bias from cream silk.

2 Place the three pieces right sides facing and stitch together to make a three-sided bauble, leaving a small gap for turning. Turn inside out and stuff firmly. Slipstitch the opening.

3 Make a loop from gold cord and stitch it to the top. Stitch gold braid centrally over each seam.

4 Trace the panel template, cut three panels from gold lamé. Stitch the panels on centrally, between the gold braid, using a fabric glue which dries invisibly.

5 Stitch a red sequin into the centre of each panel, with small pearl bead. Stitch gold sequins and pearl beads in the panels, above and below the red sequins. Stitch green sequins and pearl beads above and below the gold panels. Carefully, using invisible thread, whip stitch the thicker gold cord round each panel, oversewing the ends at the base. If necessary, secure the ends using a small drop of glue.

6 Make a tassel by winding narrow gold cord over a piece of card 55mm (2¼in) wide (see diagrams). Secure doubled gold braid around the top. Fasten off and trim ends. Stitch to base of bauble.

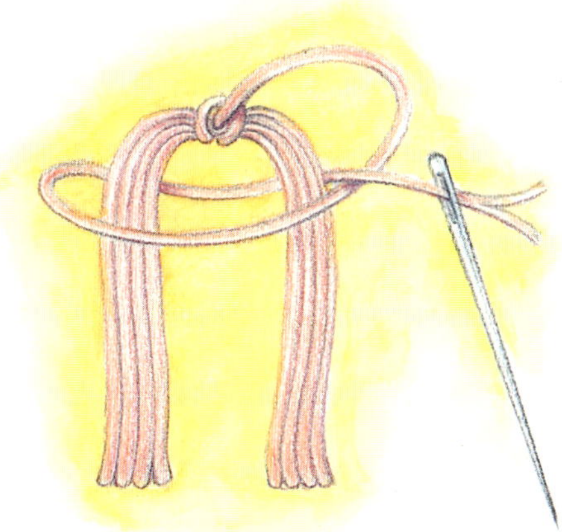

Making a tassel (b)

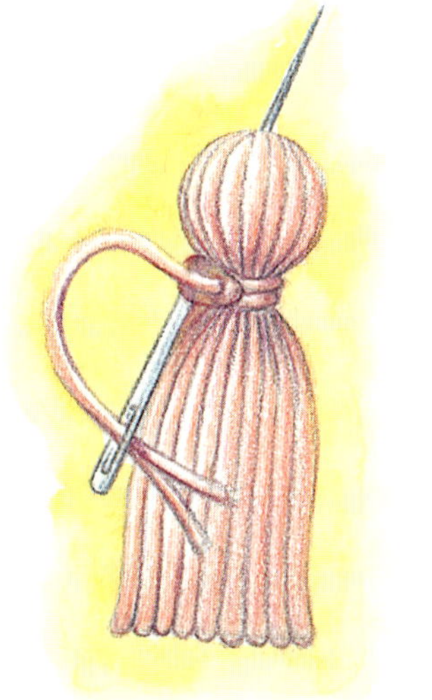

Making a tassel (c)

Christmas Traycloth

What could be nicer than being served tea or coffee in bed on Christmas morning? This bright needlepoint cloth will add an extra touch of tender loving care to start the celebrations in the happiest way. Worked in the tiniest needlepoint on fine linen, it will be appreciated by mothers, daughters and grandmothers for the thoughtful wishes it expresses. The cloth shown here has been worked over one thread on 28-count fabric, but the design would also be most effective in cross stitch on a lower count Aida or Penelope fabric, as a corner motif for a Christmas cushion or tablecloth.

MATERIALS

1 pack of Charles Craft evenweave linen in 'ivory'
matching all-purpose sewing thread
embroidery ring
size 8 embroidery needle
size 10 sharps needle
tape measure
DMC stranded cotton (floss), 1 skein each, as listed in the key

1 Measure and fold over a 1cm (½in) hem on all four sides of the square of linen. Baste in place and secure by slipstitching using tiny oversewing stitches. Remove basting stitches and press on wrong side.

2 In the bottom left-hand corner of the cloth, measure in approximately 12cm (4¾in) from each edge and mark this point with a needle. This is the starting point for your design.

3 Following the chart given on page 107, stitch the design in tent stitch using two strands of thread over one thread of fabric. As the work is very fine, great care must be taken when counting. Always be sure to start and finish off by running the end of the thread under a few stitches already worked to keep the back of the work as tidy as possible.

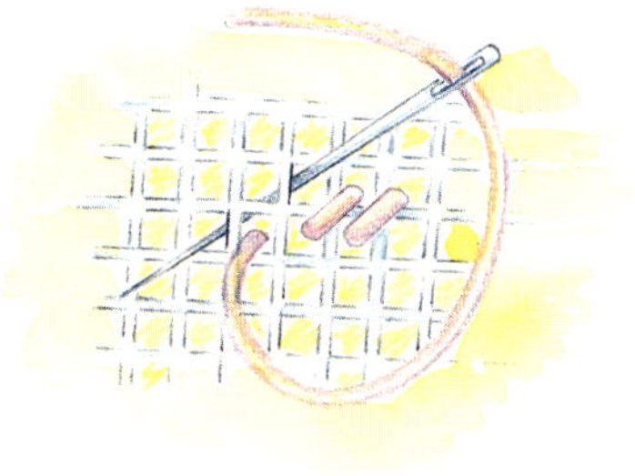

Continental tent stitch (a)

Continental tent stitch (b)

4 When the design is completed, snip off any long tails of thread and steam press the design, on the wrong side, on to a soft towel. The steam will shrink the linen slightly, making the stitches stand out crisply against the fabric.
If the traycloth is to be given as a gift, then it can be rolled carefully and put back into the original packaging before being gift wrapped.

Needlepoint or tent stitch was originally worked using woollen threads to create wall-hangings and upholstery in large country houses and palaces. Designed to produce a firm, draught-proof fabric, it was an ideal way to add protective insulation, while also making a rich decoration for austere and bare stone walls. Since its early beginnings needlepoint has remained popular, even in today's centrally heated environments, providing as it does a hard-wearing and versatile form of stitchcraft.

KEY

DMC stranded cotton (floss)

▲	**Mid brown**	**869**
И	**Mid caramel**	**977**
●	**Dark cream**	**3033**
⦸	**Mid leaf green**	**937**
▬	**Light leaf green**	**470**
T	**Bright red**	**606**
□	**Dark red**	**321**
V	**Mid rust**	**3777**
X	**Light caramel**	**435**
↑	**Orange**	**722**
△	**Dark brown**	**801**
S	**Fawn**	**738**
/	**Light coffee**	**3782**

CROSS-STITCH CHRISTMAS SAMPLER

The sampler design given here is based on early designs used in Massachusetts at the time of the American Revolution. It is stitched on a 28-count evenweave linen and therefore requires a great deal of skill and patience to achieve a good result. If such a fine linen is too difficult for you (or your eyesight), it could be changed to a larger-scale linen, though this will give a larger finished sampler. The embroidery threads have been shaded to produce the uneven colouring associated with old samplers. For an authentic aged effect, dye the linen using either an old-fashioned tea or coffee method, or one of the newer cold-water chemical dyes, which are colour fast and more stable. Many workers in the past dyed their fabrics using tea and coffee which gives a subtle, aging effect.

MATERIALS

38 x 46cm (15 x 18in) of Charles Craft 28-count even weave 100% linen in white
rectangular embroidery frame
mounting card
wooden frame
Anchor stranded cotton, as listed in the key

MEASUREMENTS
Finished size of embroidery: 32.5 x 34.5cm (12¾ x 13½in)

1 Make a narrow hem along all edges of the fabric. Mount on a rectangular embroidery frame.

2 Traditionally, samplers were stitched from one corner. Either adopt this method or find the centre of the fabric and start to embroider from the central motif. Refer to the Key for the colours of stranded cotton to be used and work all stitches using two strands of stranded cotton over two threads of linen. If the recommended threads are unavailable, refer to the conversion chart on page 124 for alternatives.

3 When you have stitched all the motifs within the border, add your own dates and initials as appropriate. Now go on to stitch the border around the whole sample.

4 When the work is completed, wash only if it has become soiled, following the manufacturer's instructions carefully. Otherwise, lay it face down on the ironing board on a soft towel and wet with a spray or damp cloth. Then iron dry. This will allow the linen to shrink slightly, making the stitches stand up.

5 Take to a reputable professional for stretching and framing, or stretch, mount and frame the picture yourself, using the materials listed.

J J
25.12.95

Key

Anchor stranded cotton (floss)

Symbol	Colour	Number
K	Dark leaf green	861
S	Burgundy red	43
И	Dark olive green	846
➘	Grey	235
●	Golden brown	375
V	Brown	889
\	Light grey blue	849
X	Mid grey blue	922
/	Creamy beige	832
←	Darkest brown	359
▬	Mid green	859
+	Dusky pink	895
T	Dark peach	338
▽	Lighter green	858

The first samplers were worked on long thin strips of hand-woven material, usually linen, which became a permanent worksheet of stitches and designs. Over the years their main purpose changed, as they became a teaching aid for the young. The rows of stitches helped pupils to memorise the alphabet and numbers. It was not until the middle of the 17th century that workers began to value their samplers sufficiently to add their names and ages.

TOOLS AND MATERIALS

Basic tools and equipment
Most craft workers will already own the equipment necessary for working the projects in this book. A full list of requirements for each individual design can be found under the relevant headings. However, it may be worth checking your workbox to ensure that you have all the necessary basic tools and that they are in good order, before commencing work.

It is, of course, essential that your crochet hooks and knitting needles are of good quality, rustless and not bent or damaged in any way. This is particularly true of fine knitting needles, which can be easily bent during use, especially when working with a tight tension. If in any doubt, do invest in new hooks and needles. For a relatively small outlay, you can be sure that your work will be of a high quality.

The normal range of embroidery frames, needles, pins, scissors and thimbles will be required for working the sewing and embroidery projects in this book. Should any unusual equipment be required, this will be specified in the specific instructions. As with crochet hooks and knitting needles, do check that everything is in good order before beginning work and, if necessary, replace any item that is damaged or unsuitable.

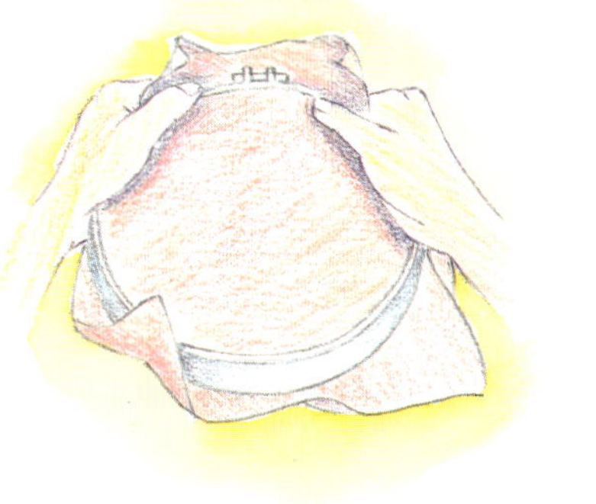

Using an embroidery hoop (a)

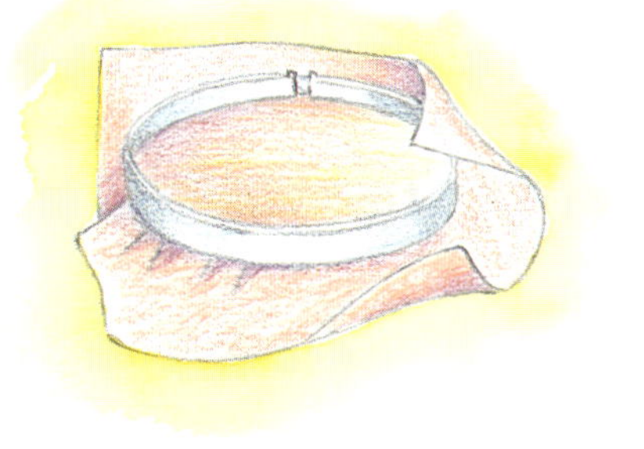

Using an embroidery hoop (b)

Specialist equipment
Toy making
For teddy bear making, it will be necessary to equip yourself with either a safety tool for assembling eyes and joints or a large empty cotton reel, which can be used to force the washers into position. A large, strong darning needle will also be required, as well as a selection of curved upholstery needles, which will make attaching ears and embroidering features on faces a little easier.

The woodwork involved in making a hobby horse is fairly basic and can easily be tackled at home, using a small saw, an electric drill and some wood glue. However, if in any doubt, consult your local handyman, who will be able to assemble the body, wheels and hand grips simply and in a very short time.

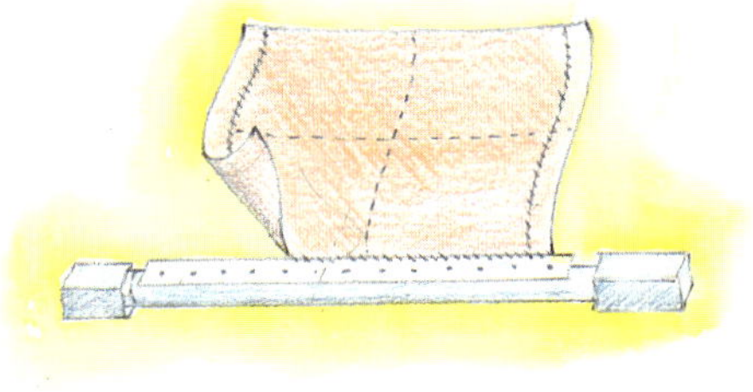

Using a slate frame (a)

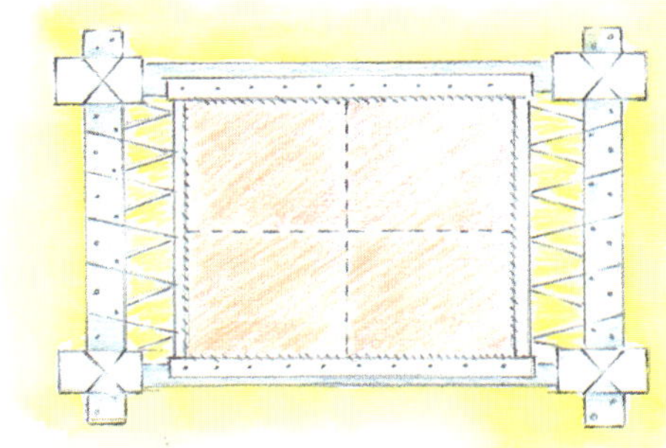

Using a slate frame (b)

Sewing aids
To aid you in your work, you may like to include the following in your workbox. These items are not essential, but can prove useful.

Use a seam ripper for careful unpicking of mis-sewn seams and embroidery, but do take care not to damage the background fabric.

When working on fine-count linen or Aida, a magnifying glass, which can be attached to a table or hung around the neck, can be very useful; as is a daylight bulb, which can be inserted into a table or anglepoise lamp. This will help differentiate between similar shades of embroidery silk when working at night.

Most workboxes contain a pincushion of some description, but it is advisable to invest in an emery bag for storing needles and pins when not in use for any length of time. This will prevent rusting and keep tips sharp.

When reading from a cross-stitch or needlepoint chart, a magnetized ruler can be a great help. It is designed to be held in position on the chart, enabling you to keep track of your place, thus preventing unnecessary mistakes.

Materials and threads

When working any of the projects in this book, always buy the best-quality fabrics that your budget will allow. The time and effort involved in making an heirloom gift does deserve only the best. Not only will the finished gift be more attractive, but the pleasure to be derived from working with the finest materials will far outweigh the extra cost involved. These projects have been designed to become treasured possessions, which, with care, will last for generations. So take the time and trouble to make them the very best you can.

Specialist fabrics

For embroidery and appliqué can often be obtained by searching through remnant and rummage bins in department stores and needlework sales. Keep an open mind when choosing fabrics and, if something unusual catches your eye, do buy it. Fabrics can be put away for future use. It is far easier to go to your fabric drawer when beginning a new project, than to trudge around the shops looking for 'something special'. The same

applies, of course, to knitting yarns and embroidery threads. There is great pleasure in sorting out and choosing just the right materials for a special project, knowing that everything you need is at your fingertips.

Silk threads for embroidery, crochet and knitting

All the silk threads used in this book are to be used straight from the spool. You will find that the thickness varies considerably. This will give added depth to your embroidery. If you wish to convert the recommended silk threads to

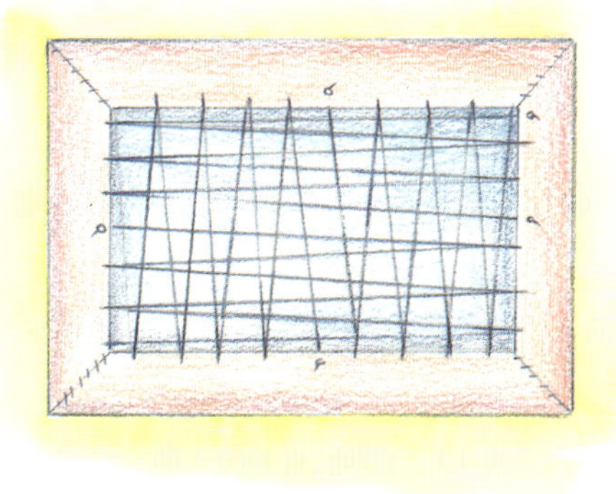

Stretching embroidery

stranded cotton, the number of strands to be used can be found in the conversion chart on pages 122-124.

Cotton and woollen threads for cross-stitch, needlepoint and surface embroidery

Unless otherwise stated, three strands of cotton thread should be used when working the designs in this book. If the specific thread colours recommended are not available, substitute the best colour match from another manufacturer.

In addition, you will require a selection of all-purpose sewing threads, tacking threads and heavy-duty nylon thread for toy making.

To help you in your choice, a list of recommended suppliers and stockists has been included on page 125-126. They will be happy to advise you on the range of goods they have available. Many of these suppliers have a mail order service, but in most cases, they will be able to give you the name of a local stockist in your area.

Templates

CHRISTENING ROBE

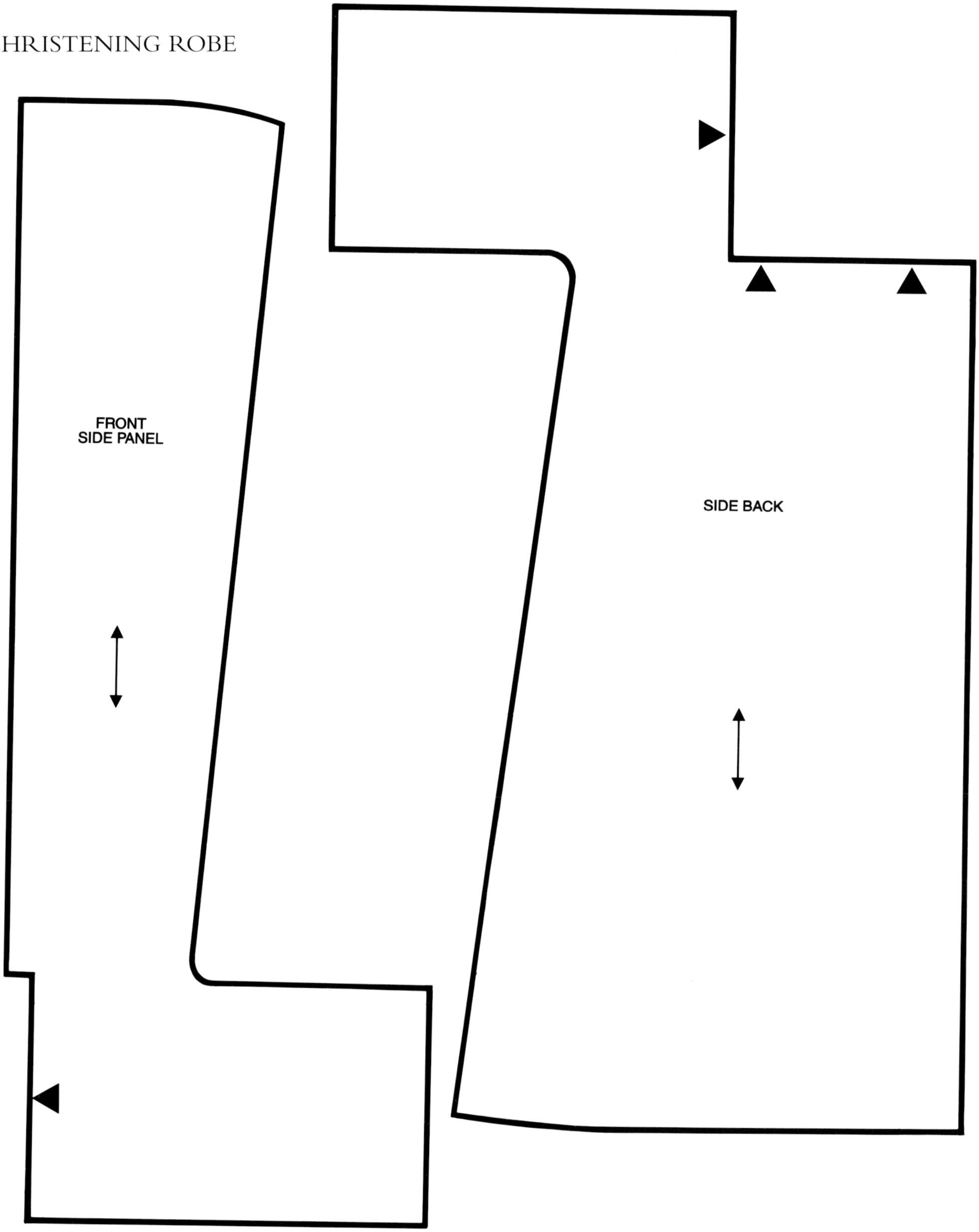

HOBBY HORSE

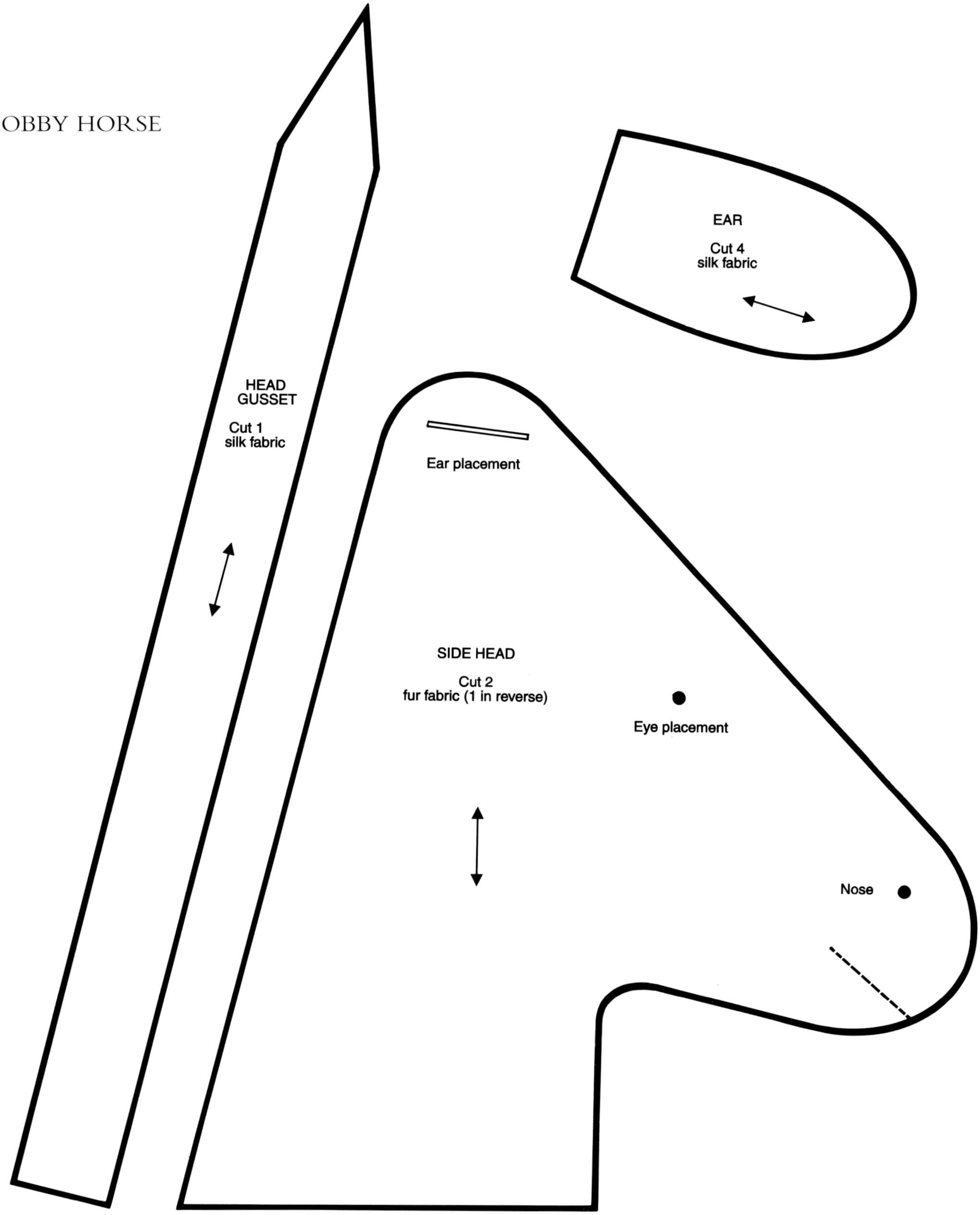
EAR
Cut 4
silk fabric
HEAD
GUSSET
Cut 1
silk fabric
Ear placement
SIDE HEAD
Cut 2
fur fabric (1 in reverse)
Eye placement
Nose

TEDDY BEAR

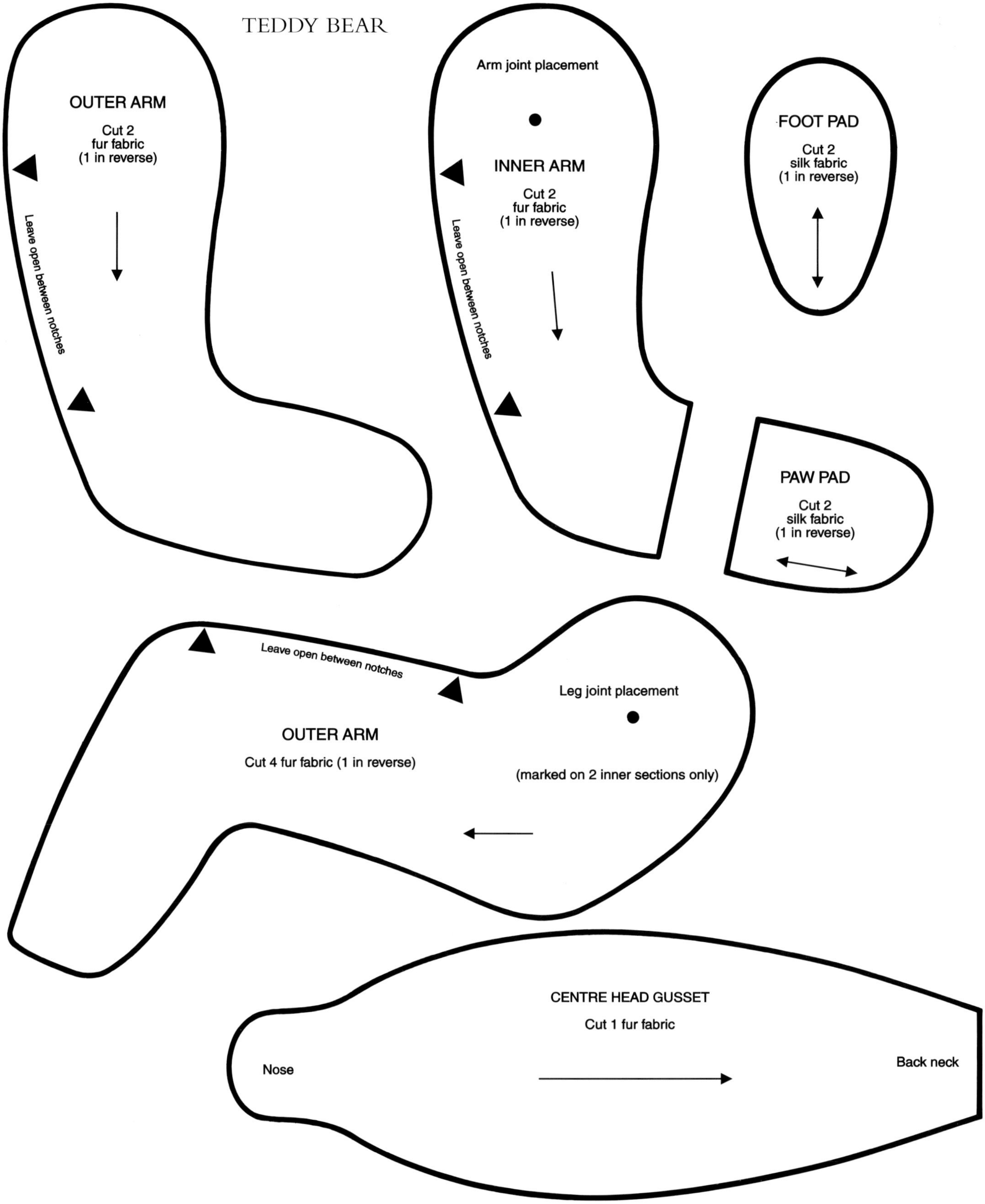
OUTER ARM
Cut 2
fur fabric
(1 in reverse)
Leave open between notches
Arm joint placement
INNER ARM
Cut 2
fur fabric
(1 in reverse)
Leave open between notches
FOOT PAD
Cut 2
silk fabric
(1 in reverse)
PAW PAD
Cut 2
silk fabric
(1 in reverse)
Leave open between notches
OUTER ARM
Cut 4 fur fabric (1 in reverse)
Leg joint placement
(marked on 2 inner sections only)
CENTRE HEAD GUSSET
Cut 1 fur fabric
Nose
Back neck

PATCHWORK ALBUM COVER

TEDDY BEAR

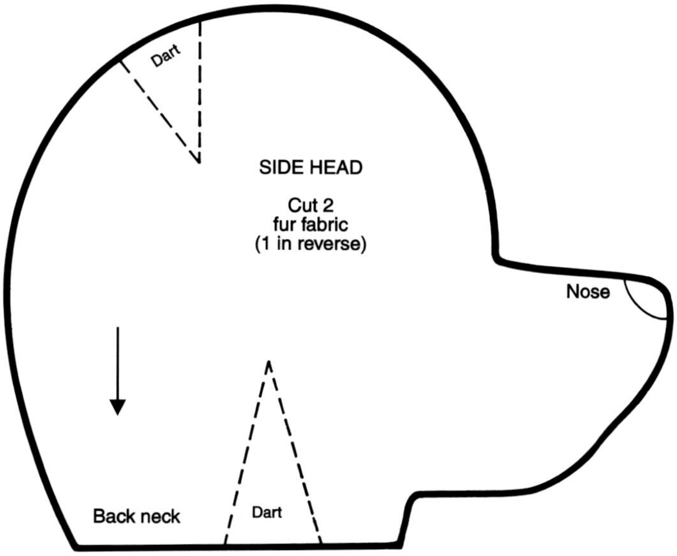

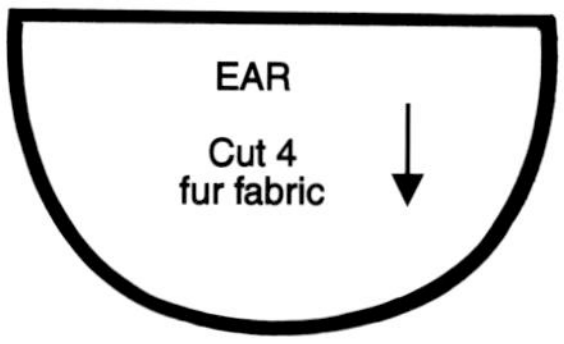

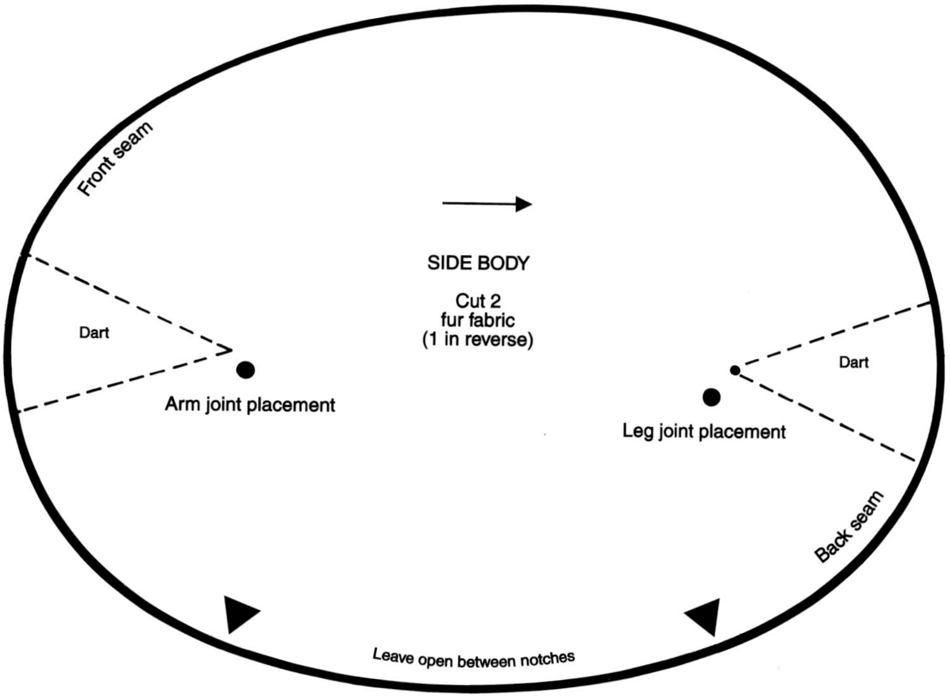

DURHAM QUILTED CUSHION

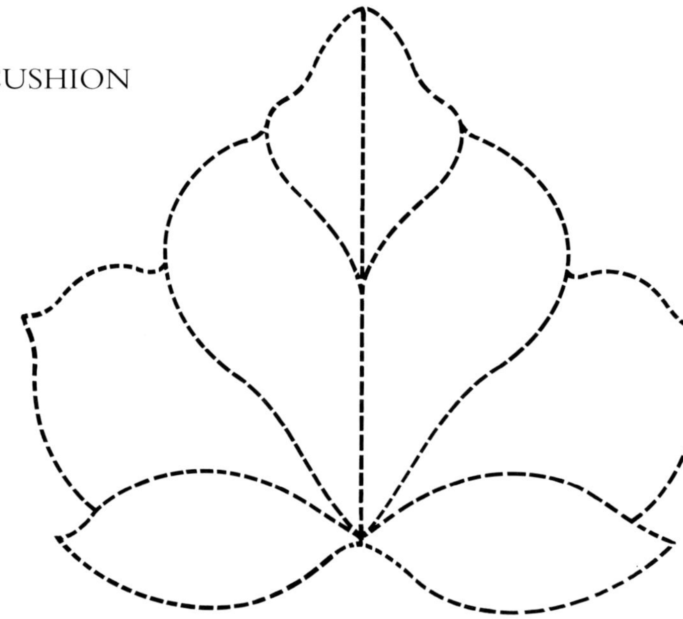

CHRISTMAS DECORATIONS

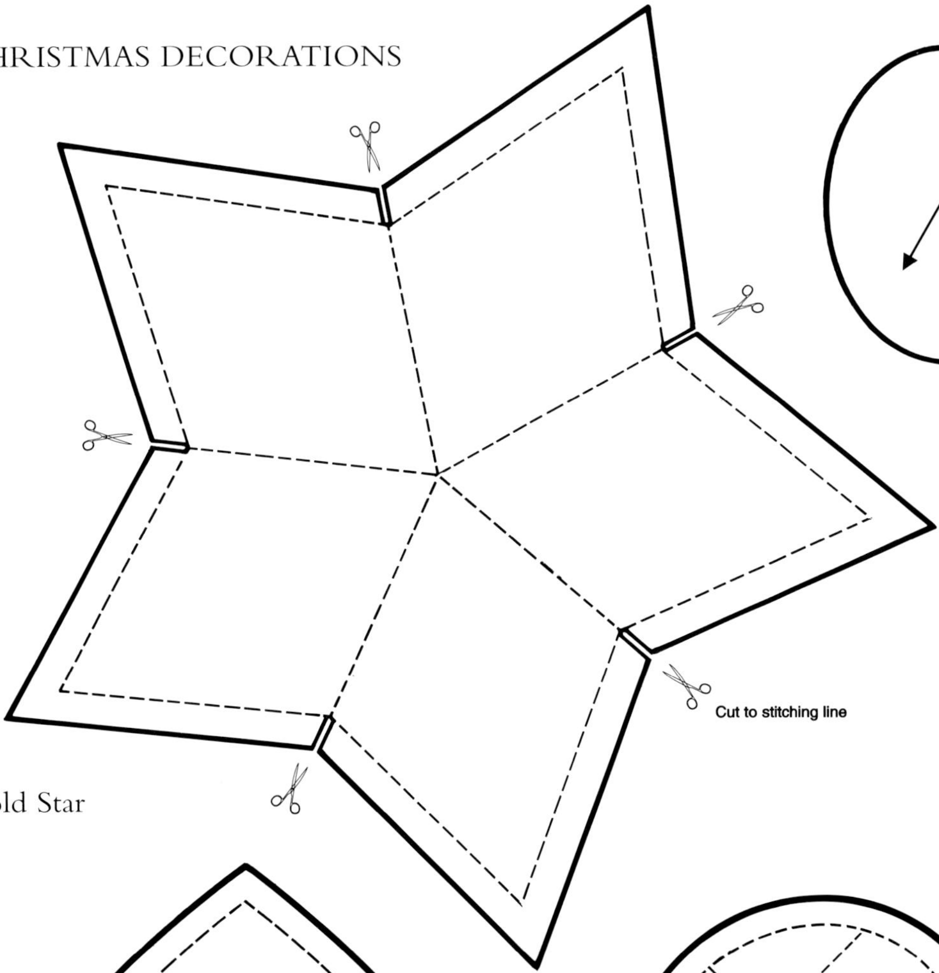

Gold Star

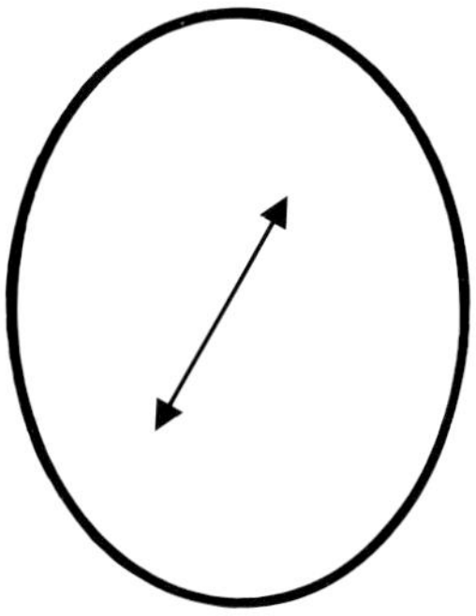

Gold, Red and Green Ball

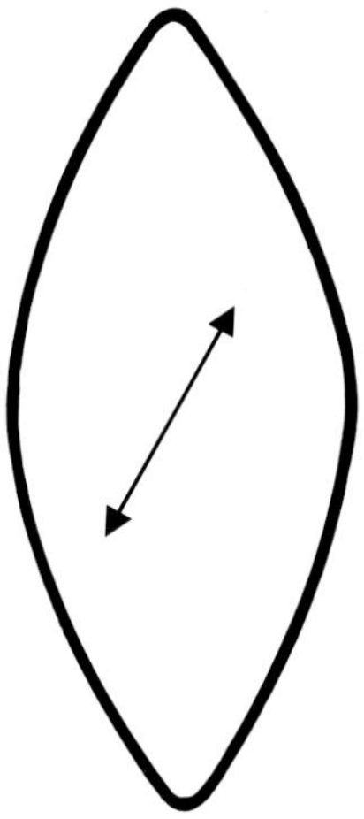

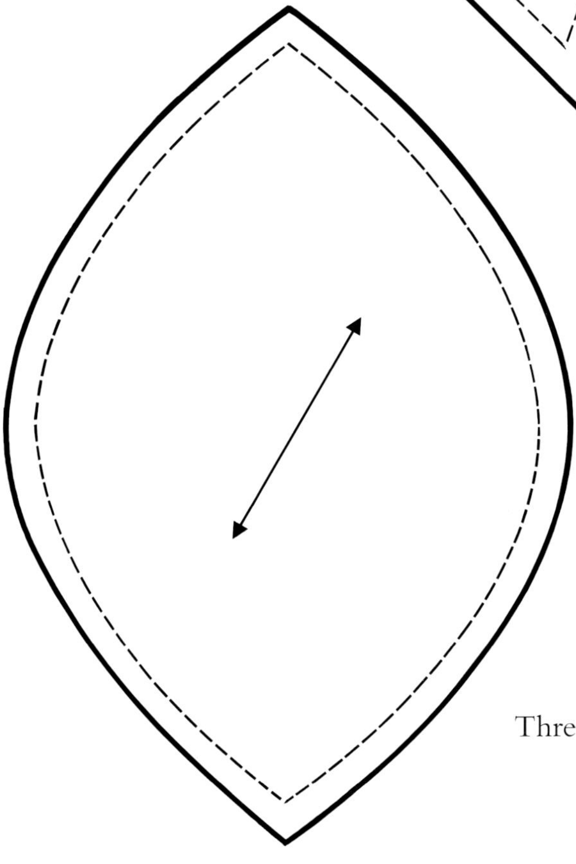

Three-sided Bauble

Red Suede Heart

Abbreviations and Conversion Charts

UK/US CROCHET TERMS AND ABBREVIATIONS

UK	USA
ch = chain	ch = chain
dc = double crochet	sc = single crochet
tr = treble	dc = double crochet
dbl tr = double treble	tr = treble
trip tr = triple treble	trip tr = double treble
lp = loop	lp = loop
rep = repeat	rep = repeat
sp = space	sp = space
st (s) = stitches	st (s) = stitches
ss = slip stitch	ss = slip stitch
cl(s) = clusters	cl(s) = clusters
p = picot	p = picot
patt = pattern	patt = pattern

LACE GARTER: THREAD CONVERSION

Anchor	DMC
23	3689

MONOGRAMMED TOWELS: THREAD CONVERSION

Anchor	DMC	Anchor	DMC
901	729	868	353
1041	535	39	3350
305	743	845	469

CROSS STITCH NURSERY PICTURE: THREAD CONVERSION

DMC	Anchor	DMC	Anchor	DMC	Anchor
blanc	white	644	830	840	379
209	109	676	891	841	378
210	108	677	886	926	850
211	342	680	907	927	849
310	black	725	305	928	274
350	11	729	890	930	922
355	1014	738	942	931	1034
356	1013	754	1012	932	343
433	371	758	882	948	1011
434	310	760	1022	3328	1024
435	1046	761	1021	3712	1023
436	1045	822	926	3753	1031
437	362	838	381	3830	5975
471	255	839	1050		

CUTWORK TABLECLOTH: THREAD CONVERSION

DMC	Anchor	DMC	Anchor
blanc	blanc	309	42
320	215	369	1043

SPRING POSY FOOTSTOOL: THREAD CONVERSION

Anchor	DMC	Anchor	DMC	Anchor	DMC
blanc	blanc	8116	7434	8156	7740
9102	7345	8776	7313	8124	7741
9644	7489	8632	7318	8118	7973
8588	7711	9100	7344	8112	7471
8154	7437	9104	7346	8628	7314
8120	7742	8594	4242	9112	7382

EMBROIDERED PANEL OF GOLDEN ROSES: THREAD CONVERSION

Mulberry Silks	DMC	Anchor	Mulberry Silks	DMC	Anchor
E104	725 (1 str)	305 (1 str)	W586	3712 (1 str)	868 (1 str)
E102	973 (1 str)	297 (1 str)	S653	928 (3 str)	274 (3 str)
S165	761 (3 str)	23 (3 str)	K506	524 (3 str)	858 (3 str)
S27	746 (3 str)	275 (3 str)	S300	741 (3 str)	303 (3 str)
F326	3078 (3 str)	293 (3 str)	F397	471 (2 str)	844 (2 str)
S412	782 (3 str)	308 (3 str)	S355	3053 (2 str)	843 (2 str)
W327	445 (1 str)	288 (1 str)	S432	580 (2 str)	924 (2 str)
S325	727 (3 str)	295 (3 str)	W596	936 (2 str)	846 (2 str)
K846	3328 (1 str)	1013 (1 str)	S398	3051 (1 str)	269 (1 str)
W587	760 (1 str)	1022 (1 str)	F932	742 (1 str)	302 (1 str)

For a non-translucent effect, the silk gauze can be replaced with 1 pack 'Charles Craft' 28-count evenweave linen in cream or 352 x 352cm (14 x 14in) of Zweigart 28-count evenweave Annabelle fabric in cream. In this case, the completed panel should be stretched and mounted in the normal manner, omitting the use of a backing fabric.

CHRISTMAS TRAYCLOTH: THREAD CONVERSION

Anchor	DMC	Anchor	DMC
869	944	1002	977
390	3033	1044	937
267	470	46	606
47	321	1014	3777
901	435	1003	722
359	801	372	738
392	3782		

CROSS STITCH CHRISTMAS SAMPLER: THREAD CONVERSION

Anchor	DMC	Anchor	DMC
861	3051	43	326
846	936	235	414
375	434	889	869
849	3752	922	930
832	3032	359	898
859	522	895	760
338	758	858	524

Zweigart 28-count half linen in off white could be substituted for the recommended Charles Craft 100% pure linen fabric which has been used to produce our sampler.

SUPPLIERS

UNITED KINGDOM

Author information
Julia Jones
PO Box 16,
Swadlincote,
Derbyshire DE12 8ZZ

For craft workshops and holidays, lectures, embroidery and craft kits. A regular newsletter is sent to readers on request. Special commissions taken for embroidery and craft work of all descriptions.

Threads
Coats Patons Crafts,
McMullen Road,
Darlington, DL1 1 YQ
Tel: 01325 381010
Fax: 01325 382300
For Anchor embroidery threads, Charles Craft Fabrics and needlework supplies. Customer helpline available to answer queries on the above telephone number. Catalogue on request.

Mulberry Silks,
2 Old Rectory Cottage,
Easton Grey,
Malmesbury,
Wilts, SN16 0PE
Tel: 01666 840881
For all high quality pure silk threads used in this book, including Golden roses panel on page 90 and silk crocheted bonnet on page 14. Designer packs available. Overseas orders welcomed.

DMC Creative World Ltd.,
Pullman Road,
Wigston,
Leicestershire LE18 2 DY
Tel: 01533 811040
Fax: 01533 813592
For local suppliers of all DMC threads, and Zweigart fabrics. Needlework catalogue available by mail order on request.

Bucilla Needlecrafts,
c/o W. Williams & Son,
Regent House,
1 Thane Villas,
London, N77 PH

Fabrics
George Weil & Sons Ltd.,
18 Hanson Street,
London, W1P 7 DB
Tel: 0171 580 3763

For mail order:
The Warehouse,
Reading Arch Road,
Redhill,
Surrey RH1 1 HG
Tel: 01737 778868
Fax: 01737 778894

Patchwork supplies
Country Threads
Patchwork and Quilting Centre
2 Pierrepont Place
Bath BA1 1JZ
Tel: 01225 480056

Piecemakers
13 Manor Green Road
Epsom KT10 8RA
Tel: 01372 743161

The Cotton Patch
1285 Stratford Road
Hall Green
Birmingham B28 9AJ
Tel: 0121 702 2840

Bear making supplies
Oakley Fabrics Ltd.,
8 May Street,
Luton,
Beds LU1 3 QY
Tel:01582 424822
Fax:01582 29362

Lace (Christening Robe and Lace Garter)
Richard Granger & Sons Ltd.,
New Tythe Mill,
Long Eaton,
Nottingham

Ribbons (Christening Robe and Lace Garter)
C. M. Offray & Sons Ltd.,
Fir Tree Place,
Church Road,
Ashford,
Middlesex, TW15 2 PH
Tel: 01784 247281
Fax:01784 245597
List of local stockists available.

Beads
Creative Beadcraft
Denmark Works
Sheepcote Dell Road
Beamond End
nr Amersham
Bucks HP7 ORX
Tel: 01494 715606

Gold braid
MacCulloch and Wallis
PO Box 3AX
25-26 Dering Street
London W1A 3AX
Tel: 0171 409 0725

Charms (Cross Stitch Nursery Picture)
Pocketful of Charms
1 Highfield Close
Malvern Link
Worcs WR14 1SH
Tel: 01684 893952

Fabric dyes
Dylon International Ltd.,
Worsley Bridge Road,
Lower Sydenham,
London SE26 5 HD
Tel: 0181 6504801
Fax: 0181 6586735.
For local stockists of fabric dyes and paints, including Cold Water Tea dyes featured on page 70, Durham Quilted cushion.

Footstool (Spring Posy Footstool)
The Stitch Shop
The Broadwalk
Port Solent
Portsmouth PO6 4TP
Tel: 01705 381049

UNITED STATES

The DMC Corporation
Port Kearney Bld.
10 South Kearney
NJ 07032-0650
Tel: 201 589 0606

Coats & Clark
PO Box 27067
Dept C01
Greenville
SC29616
Tel: 803 234 0103
The Bucilla Corporation,
1 Oak Ridge Road,
Hazleton,
PA 18201-9764
Tel: 1-800-233-3239 (toll free in USA)
Fax:1-800-453-3316 (toll free in USA)
For needlework supplies and kits, including silk embroidery ribbons. Overseas orders welcome. Catalogues available on request.

Creative Smocking,
9045 S.W. Barbur Blvd No 4,
Portland,
Oregon 97219
Tel: 503-977-3305
Fax: 503-977-3307
World s largest supplier of heirloom sewing supplies. Mail order catalogue available. Overseas orders welcome.

The Cotton Patch
Lafayette
CA 94549

Quilts & Other Comforts
1 Quilters Lane
Box 4100 Golden
CO 80402-4100
Hancocks
3841 Hinkleville Road
Paducah
KY 42001

AUSTRALIA

DMC Needlecraft Pty
PO Box 317
Earlswood 2206
NSW 2204
Tel: 02599 3088

Coats Patons Crafts
Thistle Street
Launceston
Tasmania 7250
Tel: 00344 4222

Stitching Company,
9 Pilgrim Court,
Ringwood,
Victoria 3134

The Patchwork Tree
43 Denman Street
Alderley
QLD 4051

Patchwork Affair
205 Upper Heidleberg Road
Ivanhoe
VIC 3079

Riverlea Cottage Quilts
Shop 9, 330 Unley Road
Hyde Park
South Australia 5061

NEW ZEALAND

D.D. Creative Crafts,
PO Box 74-269,
Market Road,
Auckland

ACKNOWLEDGEMENTS

The Author would like to thank the following for their help in the writing of this book:
Judi Lang for making up the Durham quilted cushion and working the fingertip towels.
Patricia Woods at Mulburry Silks for her help with silks for the crocheted silk christening bonnet, and the panel of silk roses.
DMC for providing the fabric and threads for the cutwork tablecloth.
Coats Patons Crafts for supplying the thread used for the bed throw.
Tracey Whittington, Julie Gill and the girls in the design department at Coats Patons Crafts for their help in providing the fabric and threads for the Christmas sampler and the ring box.
Judy Raine at Janet Coles Beads Ltd for her help in choosing and supplying the beads for the silk purse.
Georgina Hunt at Offray Ribbons for supplying the ribbons in the christening bonnets, christening robe and the lace garter.
Richard Granger at Richard Granger & Sons Ltd. Lace Manufacturers for supplying the lace used in the christening robe and the lace garter.
The Managing Director of George Weil & Sons for supplying the fabric for the panel of golden roses and the Durham quilted cushion.
Peter Sebastian for the woodwork involved in making the hobby horse.
And thanks to my agent, Sara Menguc, of Murray Pollinger, for her help and advice.

The Publishers would like to thank the following for their contributions to the book:
Sue Cook (cross stitch nursery picture), Jan Eaton (cutwork cherry tablecloth and napkins), Elizabeth Hunt (Christmas tree decorations), Christina Marsh (Spring posy footstool) and Christine Porter (Square dance quilt).

INDEX